ADULTING LIFE SKILLS FOR TEENS

How to Money, Budget, Bank, Pay Bills, and Everything You Need to Know About Finances

TORY HUNT

TABLE OF CONTENTS

INTRODUCTION

I never want money to dictate what I can and can't do in life." - Jessica Moorhouse.

Wear the most expensive brands.

Drive the fastest cars.

Live like a king.

Have fancy jets.

Travel around the world.

These things come to your mind when you hear the word millionaire. Am I right?

But are millionaires truly measured in these ways?

Well, it may surprise you to learn that the average millionaire does not go by these rules. They don't have this kind of lifestyle at all.

It may not look like it, but most millionaires actually live way below their means.

According to recent Census data, there are around 330 million Americans, and estimated to be 22,000,000 millionaires in the United States. This means that nearly one in every 15 people is a millionaire. It's such an astounding number!

But what may be more astounding is that many of these people do not live up to the expectation of a millionaire's lifestyle. They save about 15% of their income.

Why is that?

There are many factors involved. One of the most common reasons is that most millionaires are first-generation ones. Approximately 80% of millionaires in America are the first person in their families to be wealthy.

They were not born with a silver spoon in their mouths. They had to work hard to get where they are today. That's one of the reasons why they are modest in their ways.

I'm sure you have heard of Warren Buffett. He's a classic example of a modest, first-generation millionaire. According to Forbes, this stock market tycoon has an estimated over $100 billion net worth.

His home?

It isn't a 30,000-square-foot coastal mansion. It's an $850,000 home in a quiet Omaha, Nebraska suburb that he purchased for $31,500 in 1958.

Millionaires like Warren Buffett spend most of their lives forgoing short-term joys to achieve long-term prosperity. They have no qualms about purchasing an older used automobile, living in a modest neighborhood, and wearing affordable clothes. They have no interest in rubbing elbows with celebrities.

These choices enable these individuals to save for retirement, college, and the things they deem more important than fame and glamour. They understand that instant gratification can be enjoyable. But delayed gratification is far superior. Today's sacrifices are laying the groundwork for tomorrow's triumph.

Warren Buffett developed a knack for making money at an early age. Money matters have unfortunately been labeled an “adult” topic. But it's never too early to start enhancing your money skills.

A person's teenage years are a crucial period that can pave the way for how they view the world as an adult.

In our society, we often focus on the physical and emotional growth that occurs during the teenage years. But we should remember that it is also a time for intellectual growth, which is essential when it comes to monetary issues.

Our experiences shape how we view money. Teenagers can have vastly different financial experiences. Consider the following two examples: one teen is in financial survival mode, and the other is in financial opportunity mode.

Teenagers complain about financial issues. They constantly worry about their family not having enough money to sustain their daily needs. It's possible that their parents are only living from paycheck to paycheck.

Do *you* want to help your parents make ends meet?

Sometimes, a teen's educational goals are put to a halt because of the lack of money. A good education is what they need to get ahead at this time of their life. Unfortunately, their dreams have to be placed on the back burner.

Is education important to *you*?

There are those teens who are already earning or getting an allowance. Some don't want to go astray and don't want to be like others who blow their allowance and earnings away on trivial stuff.

Do *you* want to save *your* money and put it to good use?

Now, there are teens who feel intimidated by financial terms and concepts and want to learn more about them. They want to be experts in the complexity of money and making it grow.

Do *you* want to enhance *your* money skills?

Let's face it. Having and handling money can be complicated, and how to spend it can be even more complicated. Even at a young age, you need to have the skills to manage your money. That way, you know what to do when you get to the point that you have some financial obligations (or if you have those now).

One of the most critical lessons a teenager can have is about the value of a dollar - how to earn it, save it, and make it grow. Learning about money is critical for teenagers because it will enable them to live a prosperous life, be safe in the knowledge that they are financially secure, and have genuine respect for the worth of the money they make.

Every teen needs to be financially literate. Financial literacy refers to your capacity to comprehend and use a variety of financial concepts and abilities, such as personal financial management, budgeting, and investing. Financial literacy is the foundation of your financial relationship with money and a lifelong learning process.

Financial literacy and hard work will allow you to live the life you want for yourself and your family. Building enough savings, assets, and liquid cash will let you pamper yourself and continue the vocation of your choice without being constrained by a paycheck.

But remember that despite how things are now, you can still change them. While you may not be able to live the jet-set lifestyle you desire, you can take steps now while you are still young. You can earn, save, and grow your money, so you won't have to worry about it later.

The teenage years are the best time for a person to learn how to manage money. The fundamentals of budgeting, saving, and money management will help you become more financially self-sufficient as you get older.

However, many young people need to be taught these skills. According to a report released by the Programme for International Student Assessment, one in every five teenagers lacks basic money management skills.

But don't worry. I am here to help you.

I am writing this book to share with you what I know about managing money. I began working at an early age and have learned how valuable money is. I have experienced financial struggles that have helped me to become more prudent with my financial choices.

This topic is very important to me because I know what it is like to struggle with money. Because of these struggles, I pushed myself to become a financial expert. Now it's time that I share what I have learned and experienced.

Allow this book to be your guide. It will lead you to become money smart, a skill you need to live in this world of ever-changing norms.

This book will assist you in developing critical financial skills that will help you prepare for the future as an adult.

This book contains life-changing tips and examples to help you manage your finances. You will find a lot of advice to help you successfully navigate financial issues.

By the end of this book, I am confident that you will be able to:

*Make the most of your money

*Learn how to budget

*Learn how to earn and save to achieve your money goals

*Be more confident in managing your finances

*Fully understand how savings, investing, and borrowing work

*Know common personal finance terms

*Take responsibility for financial obligations

* Spend money wisely

*Understand many other noteworthy money lessons that can jumpstart your journey toward a fulfilling and abundant adulthood.

Financial success and freedom require both dreaming and hard work to obtain those dreams. Starting this journey at a young age will increase your financial possibilities.

Do you want to avoid becoming a person who lives paycheck to paycheck?

Do you want to lift the burden of financial difficulties off your parents' backs?

Do you want to be able to buy whatever you want whenever you want?

Do you want to help others who have financial needs?

Do you want to achieve your goals in the soonest possible time?

Do you want to become financially independent and intelligent?

Gear up! On the next pages, we will journey together and learn how to be financially smart!

Chapter One

Dangerous Money Myths

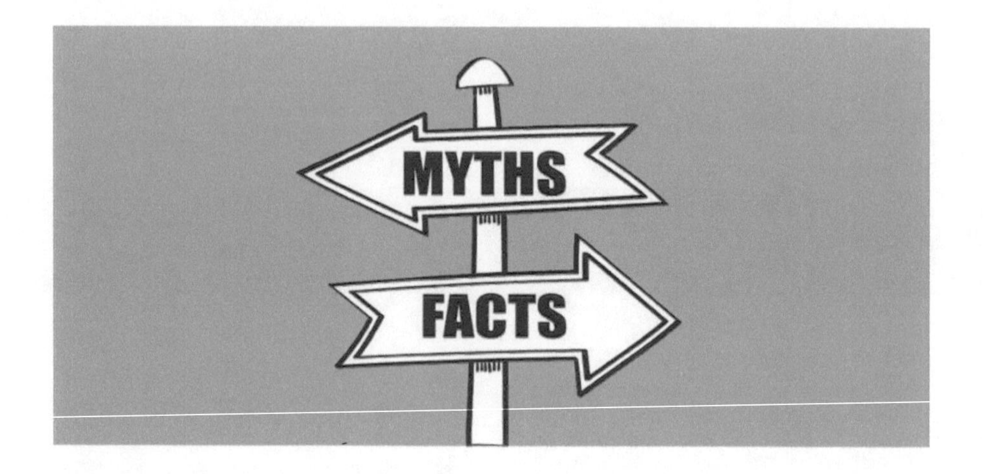

Handling money all starts in your head. Many adults continue to have false notions about money. As early as your teenage years, it's critical that you develop a healthy financial mindset and be mindful of financial matters.

There are a lot of myths about personal finance out there. Thanks to personal finance blogs, television money experts, and advice from family, friends, and neighbors, there's no shortage of money advice — how to make, manage, and increase it. With so much information coming at us from all these different sources, it can be difficult to distinguish between fact and fiction.

There are many myths out there masquerading as fact. However, the truth is that these myths are trapping people in lifelong financial struggles.

10 Money Myths You Should Stop Believing

Here are some of the most common money myths you should be aware of and work to correct:

1) Myth: Budgets are painful.

Many people get annoyed, if not outraged when the subject of budgeting comes up. They feel they earned the right to spend their money whenever and however they want.

"I'm an adult who doesn't need someone to tell me what to do or where I should spend my money," some would say.

Budgeting might feel pain because it constrains us from doing what we desire with our money.

Reality: Budgeting is an opportunity.

It's an opportunity since budgeting allows you to keep track of and limit your spending. And with that, you save more money.

Budgeting is not a pain. What's painful is a bill you are unable to pay, a loan that costs a fortune, and not having enough money for your future.

2) Myth: A credit card is just like a debit card or cash.

You rarely notice you're spending money when you use credit cards since there's a distance between making purchases and really paying for them. One of the reasons individuals overspend with credit cards is that they don't feel the agony of the purchase as much as they would if they paid cash.

Teens can spend a lot on their credit cards. Most of them assume they can pay off their charges at their leisure.

Reality: A credit card is definitely not a debit card.

A credit card is not free money. It's not like taking money out of your ATM.

When you use your credit card, it's just the beginning. Remember that you'll have to repay whatever you bought with the card. When you use a credit card, you're spending the bank's money, not your own. This money must be paid back, plus interest.

3) Myth: There's no reason to save for retirement.

At this point in your life, retirement is the farthest from your mind. You might say, "I haven't even considered what I want to do with my life yet, let alone what would happen if I retired."

Surprisingly, many people believe that after a property is paid for and they have all the necessities and luxuries they need and want, there is no longer a need for money, mainly when the individual is older.

“In retirement, Medicare will cover my medical expenses.”

“I will rely on Social Security.”

These are the arguments of those who don't feel the need to save for retirement. Are these justified?

Reality: There's every reason to save for retirement.

Early planning can make your retirement years more pleasant and pleasurable for you and your family. And it's never too early to start.

One of the most beneficial aspects of beginning your retirement planning early is that you will have plenty of time to save. This situation means that instead of trying to save a vast sum of money in a short period of time, you can afford to contribute modest amounts on a regular basis. This saving method will pile up over time, allowing you to live a more comfortable retirement.

4) Myth: Being in debt is bad.

Why do people consider debts wrong? Why do people collectively fear being in debt?

*They think debts don't add value to a person's lifestyle.

*For them, having debt adds a burden to their lives.

*Mounting interest and due dates make them apprehensive.

Debts could jeopardize your financial situation because you'll have to pay both the principal (the amount you borrowed) and the interest (the fee or charge imposed by the lender as part of your borrowing). Missed payments result in overlapping increases in penalties, worsening the debt even more.

Reality: Debts can be good.

Debts incurred through loans are regarded as good debt if you understand why you're taking them out, and they don't put you in financial distress.

You can learn more about this in Chapter 8.

5) Myth: I don't need an emergency fund.

Did you know that unexpected expenses are American's #1 financial concern? Well, that's what the Fidelity Investments New Year Financial Resolutions Study stated in 2018. But what's even more surprising is that only 39% of Americans have enough savings to cover a $1,000 emergency.

This situation boils down to the age-old thinking that an emergency fund is unnecessary. How many people have you heard bragging that they will never find themselves in an emergency? These people have this overpowering belief that nothing wrong will happen to them.

Some think savings are unnecessary because they can use their credit card anytime. Or they can take out a loan.

Yes, these are options. But are these wise choices? Won't these leave you more in debt in the long run?

Reality: Emergency funds are necessary.

Let's face it; life is full of surprises. Chances are that you will confront an unexpected expense at some point in your life. You can get sick, you might have a minor accident with the car, you can get laid off, and you can overlook some payments. Saving money is difficult, but it's even more complicated when paying off credit card debt or paying for a loan with atrocious interest. You can pay the unexpected payment if you have emergency money. You can be responsible by expecting the unexpected to happen. When it does, you won't have to worry about being unable to pay your bills. Creating and growing an emergency savings fund can give you the financial cushion to weather a financial storm in the short term.

6) Myth: Investing is only meant for the wealthy.

When the word "investment" comes up, we think of the words "capital," "costly," "premium," and many others that we associate with affluent individuals. For ordinary people, especially teenagers like yourself, the idea seems far-fetched.

Investing might be intimidating for those with little financial resources, and setting aside a large sum of money or even modest amounts can take time and effort. Most of us relate the idea of investments to colossal capital and continuous cash flow coming out of one's pockets, which is not possible for the not-so-wealthy.

Many people fantasize about becoming wealthy and investing and earning more money without putting in a lot of effort. They want to be able to save enough money to invest in what they believe in and reap the rewards afterward. However, only a tiny percentage of people truly achieve this in their lives.

Many people dream of becoming wealthy, yet many never manage to achieve their goals. This failure to achieve goals is not due to a lack of effort on their part, and it is not because they are undeserving. This situation happens to a lot of folks since they don't realize that they can invest right now.

For young people, it can be doubly hard to believe one can invest. You may be thinking that investments are way out of your league.

Reality: You can invest regardless of any financial status.

You heard that right. You may start your investment now with your money in your bank account. You don't need any unique abilities or experience, nor do you need to be wealthy. You may begin right now with whatever you have.

The most significant factor in investments is not money. It's time.

Don't disregard small amounts of money. They are only the first step in a long journey.

We'll discuss this further in Chapter 7.

7) Myth: If the price is high, the quality is high.

A branded bag or a generic one?

If one can afford it, a person picks the former. Most people believe that paying more for an item means that the item is well beyond the quality of the cheaper ones.

Some people are concerned that the low-cost items they purchase may break down or fail to perform as expected. And when that happens, here are what the majority of folks say:

"You get what you pay for!"

"Buy it right the first time. Else, you want to buy it twice."

Well, this thinking is quite logical. If something costs more to make, it is definitely priced higher.

Reality: Price has nothing to do with the quality.

Consumers' perceptions of whether a product is of high quality are heavily influenced by marketing. Price can only be used as a measure of the market's desired quality.

However, regardless of the price, a product may still be of poor value or good quality. Price has nothing to do with it.

One research study showed that the mere mention of price could easily sway the brain. Suppose a person is told they are tasting two different wines (one is $5 and the other $45). In that case, the brain's pleasure center becomes more active, and the person believes they are enjoying the more expensive vintage. As a result, the consumer will assume that the more costly wine is of higher quality just because it is more expensive.

This just shows that a higher price does not necessarily mean better quality.

8) Myth: You can only be rich if you have high salary.

Blue-collar jobs don't equate with six-figure salaries. Those with low-profile jobs think they'll never get rich.

You or your parents may know many individuals who work one full-time job and lead ordinary lives. They fantasize about having a large bank account and the lifestyle that comes with it, but they do nothing to achieve it.

A person can afford to live in a comfortable home, go on vacation a few times a year, buy new clothes as needed, and provide a good education for their children. But they will never be Oprah Winfrey.

That's what we were told. So, we accept whatever we have and turn our backs on any dreams of getting rich.

Reality: You can be wealthy regardless of your current salary.

I will not bore you with a discussion of why and how. Just read these stories:

1. Sidney Torres was working as a construction worker when he approached his mentor, who also happened to be his grandmother, for a $40,000 loan to buy an investment property in New Orleans. His grandmother required him to present a business strategy, building timetable, and financial estimates because he was no easy target.

His grandmother's no-nonsense approach and his career in the trade prepared him for the rigors of property flipping. Today, Sidney Torres is a successful entrepreneur and real estate developer. He credits his success to that first New Orleans flip. Torres served as the host of CNBC's "The Deed," a show where he used his knowledge and skill to help struggling property owners get the most out of their investments.

2. Dishwashing at a restaurant is a complex, arduous job — yet for some of the world's most famous chefs, it was a vital

stepping stone. Thomas Keller is a famed chef who attributes his success to the abilities he learned as a dishwasher, such as organization, teamwork, efficiency, and repetition.

3. Thomas Keller is an author, television personality, and serial restaurateur who founded Per Se in New York City and the French Laundry in Northern California, among other restaurants. He started as a dishwasher and worked his way up the restaurant ladder. Keller, one of the most well-known chefs, is worth $50 million.

These stories show that getting rich has nothing to do with what you are getting paid at the moment. Instead, it has to do with one's determination to succeed.

9) Myth: It's too risky to dabble in the stock market.

The stock market is complicated. Commodity, price risks, credit rating, and many other terms may scare you.

Now before you get overwhelmed, let me just point out one of the risks involved - Headline Risk.

The danger that news articles will harm a company's business is referred to as headline risk. With the never-ending flow of news, no company is immune to the risk of making the front page. For example, news of the Fukushima nuclear disaster in 2011 hurt equities in any industry that dealt with nuclear power, from uranium miners to utilities in the United States.

A single piece of bad news can trigger a market reaction against a firm, a sector, or both. Bad news on a larger scale, such as the debt crisis in some eurozone countries in 2010 and 2011, can hurt entire economies, leave alone equities, and have a noticeable impact on the global economy.

Global economy? Yikes! Understandably, these ideas can make you run in another direction.

You may ask yourself , if a company can face such risks, how will one person fare?

Reality: The stock market is Risk and Return.

Well, let me be honest. Investing in stocks *can* be risky. However, there is another point to consider is the return on investment.

If you must know, despite the risks involved, each saving and investment option comes with its own set of rewards. The ease with which investors receive their money when they need it, the rate at which their money will increase, and the safety of their money are all factors to consider.

Because they are federally insured, insured money market accounts and stocks are safe. If you need money for whatever reason, you can easily access it from your savings account.

The most prevalent investing products are stocks, bonds, and mutual funds. All of these products have larger risks and possible rewards than savings accounts. Stocks have consistently delivered the highest average rate of return over several decades.

10) Myth: I'm not making enough money to save.

Some people find that there is no breathing room on a tight budget. They live from paycheck to paycheck. They already worry about stretching their budgets. Where in the world would they find some money to set aside?

It is impossible to save when your expenses exceed your income. Right now, some of you may be starting off with part-time jobs, which pay very little. You can't save money when you spend more than you earn.

"I can't save money because I don't make enough" is a common complaint.

It's true that there's only so much you can do in terms of cost-cutting. There are times when you've reduced your costs to the bare minimum, and still, there's not much left.

But all of this doesn't necessarily mean that you don't have an opportunity to save.

Reality: You can increase your income and can finally save.

You can't just wait and watch life pass you by. You can't always wallow in self-pity that you don't have enough money, that you are unable to save for a rainy day.

When you prioritize saving, you can find ways to increase your income to save. And there's always some unnecessary expense you can give up.

Even if it's a modest amount, saving something trains the muscle so that the habit is already set when your financial circumstances improve. Plus, modest sums can build up, and having money saved is preferable to having none at all!

Next Steps

What do you think of the above money myths? Do you believe them? It's not easy to let go of certain beliefs, especially if these beliefs have been ingrained since childhood.

I recommend that you reflect on your past beliefs about money and see how much they connect to the myths mentioned above. You can write them down if you want.

Then, you can read the chapter once more and see how all these myths mess with your ideas about money.

After reading all about these myths, several questions may come to your mind. One of them could be:

I'm still young, so why should I stress myself out over money?

However, today's a good time to start thinking about money matters.

The money myths shared are not comprehensive. There are others you can check online to help you better understand what you should and should not believe about money.

It’s best to find out on your own the truth about money. That way, you can form your own opinion and make the right decisions.

And of course, it's very important to take action about money. Even at your age, one of the most crucial things you can do is to begin making it.

Chapter Two

Making Your First Dollar

Teenagers used to have part-time jobs all the time, whether it was helping to pack bags at the shop, babysitting, or delivering newspapers. However, it is becoming increasingly unusual these days. Experts in the marketplace are concerned about the reluctance of teenagers to work part-time or summer jobs, which has become a national trend. Why is this happening, and how will it affect your long-term future?

In the United States in 2020, approximately 17.6 percent of teenagers between the ages of 16 and 19 were employed while enrolled in school. This represents a decrease from the previous year when 19.2 percent of teenagers worked while attending school.

Teens' lack of enthusiasm for working is sad because working part-time teaches work ethic and soft skills from an early age. Although it may appear unrelated, scooping ice cream or working in retail can help you become a better doctor, accountant, teacher, or person in any other profession.

It will help if you take advantage of the opportunities in front of you. Unlike before, there are many jobs, apart from delivering newspapers, babysitting, and mowing lawns for you.

Why work when you're still a student?

Here are reasons why you should consider getting a job now:

1) It gives you a much broader view of life, and interacting with people you might not otherwise encounter is a fantastic eye-opener to the world.
2) It promotes a growing sense of financial independence and appreciation for money. Nothing teaches a teenager to respect money and the genuine worth of the goods they buy, like spending their own money to get what they want. The weeks or months of saving, the patience required, the sacrifice of other purchases along the way—all of this is a vital lesson that will prepare people for their future as responsible adults capable of functioning successfully in the adult world.

As you earn money and then spend it, this is the ideal moment where you will learn about financial responsibility.

Especially when your parents tell you to contribute to anything little, such as your food or transportation expenses, creating budgets, and learning how much gasoline costs. A single paycheck may teach you all of these things.

3) It aids in the development of social skills. As a teenager, getting a part-time job can be extremely beneficial to their social skills. Workplaces introduce young people to coworkers who are often of varying ages and backgrounds. Being the "young person" and having to interact with folks who are decades older might be intimidating. It's possible you have never experienced anything like it before.

If you work in the service industry, you will most likely interact with a wide spectrum of consumers who are diverse not only in age but also in personality type. Interacting with individuals from different walks of life is a valued talent. You will be better prepared for a wide range of future occupations and situations if you have strong social skills. A young person with high social skills can appear more confident, which can help them in a variety of situations.

4) Working introduces a level of self-control that many young people are unfamiliar with. Their primary obligation may have been getting to school on time or turning in homework before the deadline until now. However, being late for work has more negative implications than being late for school, such as lost salary and, in the worst-case scenario, job termination.

Much part-time employment necessitates getting up early on weekends or altering social plans to accommodate work obligations. This is all fantastic practice that will benefit you in the future by instilling a mature, responsible mindset that will appeal to potential employers.

5) To learn how to find balance. While juggling school, extracurricular activities, and jobs, you will learn that it takes a lot of organization and sacrifice to keep all of your obligations. Teens who work while attending school discover how difficult it is to be an adult with many obligations. It's a great time to explore and learn how to manage your life while you're still young and have parental assistance.

You'll improve your ability to deal with rejection. It's possible that you won't obtain the first job you apply for. Rejection is a part of life that can be difficult to deal with. The more rejection we endure, the easier it gets to move forward and recover.

6) It boosts one's self-confidence. Many of you struggle with self-confidence, especially in unexpected situations. Older folks may have become accustomed to feeling apprehensive; but still having to complete a task or event, a teenager's first instinct may be to avoid it.

Having a job means that most people will be confronted with responsibilities or situations that are intimidating, at least at first. However, avoiding work is rarely an option, and most individuals discover that once they've become accustomed to a scenario or learned and performed a task a few times, their nervousness dissipates, and they're left with a new ability.

Learning how to deal with a variety of situations and duties, no matter how 'simple' they may appear, allows you to gain confidence and develop as a person while also better preparing yourself for the future. Many occupations and situations require an inner sense of self-assurance. Thus getting some early experience is beneficial.

7) It improves self-esteem. Earning your own money and being able to deal with a variety of situations and individuals can improve a young person's self-esteem. Not having to rely on your parents for financial support instills a sense of responsibility and self-worth, as well as the freedom to make your own decisions.

Not only that. It also allows you to help others by allowing you to select gifts for family members for birthdays and Christmas, as well as donate to any organizations you care about. It's a well-known fact that helping others makes people feel better about themselves.

1) While you're young, it's a good idea to start learning about how difficult it is to find work; it's a major concern, but the stakes aren't as high. Teens can learn skills like filling out an application, producing a strong résumé, and giving a successful interview by looking for jobs at an early age. Honing all of these talents while you are still young can help you better prepare for the future when you need to locate a career-launching job.

2) You'll improve your interviewing abilities. The more jobs you apply for, the better at interviewing you will become. Learning how to conduct a successful interview is a valuable life skill. It can assist you in gaining college admission and possibly landing a full-time career.
3) It provides opportunities. The best reason from a teenager's point of view is that having a job provides opportunities and a new sense of freedom. With your very own money, you can buy things that your parents might not like or can't afford.

You can purchase concert tickets; go to the movies with your pals without having to ask for money; buy those expensive shoes and clothes you want; start a new hobby; take up driving lessons and eventually own a car; even save money to travel abroad when you are old enough.

Having a job gives a teenager more options and opens up a wider range of possibilities. They can say 'yes' when asked to socialize with friends without having to wait for their parents to agree to pay for it. Even when they earn money by completing tasks at home, many of the things they desire to spend money on considerably exceed the usual allowance.

Getting your first job can assist you in resolving this problem. Having work experience on a Curriculum Vitae (CV) or a Resume is beneficial in the long run when applying for future changes, whether that be another employment or a course of study. It denotes a resourceful, self-sufficient, and a motivated young individual who will be a valuable asset to a company or organization.

Now that we discussed the benefits of having a part-time job, here are some things to take into consideration before looking for your first job.

1) Location is critical to be able to go to work quickly and without too much stress. Not only will you be more likely to show up because you won't miss the third bus, but it will also put you in a better mood while you're at work. Since you are still a teen you should also find a job where the location is safe and there's a close route to your home.
2) Make sure the job you're applying for is a good fit for your schedule. It won't work if the job demands you to work a morning shift while you're in class. Try to find a career that you will be able to manage with your studies.
3) Before you apply, make a note of what kind of experience is required for the position. CPR training, for example, is required to work as a lifeguard. Some pools provide training, while others do not. It's like applying for a waitress position without ever having eaten at the restaurant. Isn't it crazy?
4) Last but not least, consider what kind of experience you want to have. You probably won't want to be a grocery store cashier if you believe stocking shelves is the worst thing you could do. There are a lot of choices out there, so pick one that doesn't make you want to vomit every time you think about it.

There are many jobs available for teens. Here are some part-time jobs for you to consider:

Part-time employment

1) Cashier in a Juice/Smoothie Shop.

The only thing you should know before starting this job is how to avoid sticking your hand in a blender. Perhaps a little basic math as well. You get to combine fruit to prepare someone's breakfast or snack time drink. You'll also get to sample the icy delights of smoothies while obtaining crucial cash-handling skills.

2) Front Desk/Reception at a Salon/Spa.

Do you have the ability to multitask? Do you have excellent interpersonal skills? Client greetings, scheduling, and answering the phone are all responsibilities of the front desk staff. You can also be in charge of product sales and giving tours to new or prospective customers. According to the Bureau of Labor Statistics, receptionists earn a median hourly wage of $14.01.

3) Lifeguards

Many teenagers like working as lifeguards at their neighborhood pool or beach. Despite the fact that they must complete a particular training program in order to be certified, many teenagers find this job satisfying, especially if they enjoy being outside.

4) Car wash attendant

As a car wash attendant, you will be in charge of washing, buffing, and shining a car. On average, one can earn about $10 per hour.

5) Daycare assistant

You will be tasked to care for the kids in daycare. Also known as daycare aides, these people help young children by changing their diapers, potty-training them, feeding them, engaging them in fun activities, and reading books to them.

6) Concession stand worker

If you get hired, you will operate the concession stalls. Your primary tasks are to give food and drinks to attendees at various events. You'll collect drink and food orders from customers, as well as process payments and changes. Workers at concession stands are also responsible for keeping the area clean and pleasant.

7) Barista

In a coffee shop, a barista prepares coffee-related beverages for customers. To make delectable cocktails, they will follow and memorize particular instructions. Baristas are also responsible for greeting clients, answering any questions they may have regarding the menu, taking inventory, and keeping the lobby area clean for customers. The pay is approximately $11 per hour.

8) Camp counselor

Although this job is typically available only during the summer, it's a great stepping stone for work. Camp counselors work closely with campers to ensure that they are safe and have a good time. These people will collaborate with other counselors to arrange activities and events that will keep kids engaged. Other responsibilities include ensuring that campers adhere to regulations and procedures, managing any conflicts among kids, and cleaning certain areas of the camp.

9) House-cleaner

Cleaning houses or individual rooms is the responsibility of house cleaners. This includes sweeping and vacuuming, washing clothes and dishes, and dusting and wiping surfaces, much like your mother presumably makes you do at home.

10) Resort desk clerk

In resorts, work surges during the summer, and they frequently hire teenagers to assist with the extra work. For your assistance, you might earn roughly $12 per hour.

11) Delivery driver

You will frequently be in charge of carefully delivering goods or food products without causing damage to the contents. The national average salary for this is $16.81 per hour.

12) Library assistant

One of the more lucrative jobs for teens, this pays around $13 per hour. Library assistants will assist visitors in finding books and checking them out. They'll also help librarians with inventory, shelving, and digitizing printed files and older documents.

13) Restaurants/catering

Working in restaurants and catering establishments is great for full-time students. The hours and shifts are flexible, and there is the opportunity to make extra money through tips. On a busy shift in London restaurants, servers can expect to earn roughly £50 ($69). It's even better in the United States, where consumers expect to be tipped.

14) Retail sales associate

This job is a fantastic option for teenagers. For $13.13 an hour (approximate), teenagers are expected to stock shelves or assist clients.

15) Package sorter

Package sorters may be required to sort inventory or prepare things for transportation, depending on the warehouse.

16) Golf caddy

Carrying players' clubs between holes pays $18.35 per hour in this position. This is an hourly rate that can vary by state.

17) Movie theater employee

This is kind of a broad description because the tasks include taking tickets, manning the concession stands, and cleaning up after movies.

18) House Sitter/Caretaker

One of the best aspects of being a home sitter or caretaker is that you don't have to do much other than ensure that the property you're watching is safe and secure. If there is a problem, you may need to schedule repairs as well as do routine maintenance. It's not much different than hanging out at home when you're working for the proper client. This relatively easy job has a pleasing pay rate. According to Zippia, that rate is $27 per hour. Keep in mind, the amount may vary by state, but not by too much.

19) Customer service

A career in customer service is worth pursuing if you enjoy assisting people, fixing problems, and resolving issues. There are a variety of customer service positions available, and many of them need internet work, allowing you to work from home. You may be able to work around your day job or school schedule because the schedule is flexible. Customer service workers earn a median hourly wage of $16.23, according to the Bureau of Labor Statistics.

20) Data encoder

Data entry jobs online will pay teenagers who are 18 or 19-years-old fairly well to input data. But you would need basic software skills.

Selling/Telemarketing/Reviewer

1) Caller for Market Research/Survey

Conducting surveys or market research is one of the simplest sorts of phone calling employment. You are not obligated to sell anything. Rather, you're gathering information or asking questions for your job. According to Indeed, market research callers make an average of $12.75 per hour.

2) Call reviewer

If you're 17 or older, you can evaluate calls for quality assurance. Humanatic.com, for example, hires people to listen to recorded calls and then assess their quality.

3) Song reviewer

Sounds awesome, right? Slice The Pie, for example, pays consumers to review songs, ads, clothing, and other items. Brands, record labels, and artists can use your feedback to help develop their products before they go online.

You are compensated based on the quality of your review and the site's star rating. You'll get your money through PayPal, and you'll be able to pay out once your account hits $10.

Freelance

1) Babysitter

Babysitting jobs can be flexible, enjoyable, and profitable. They're also great experiences for those interested in education, healthcare, or social services. You can immediately apply for jobs, but you may be required to pass background checks or submit references.

2) Dog walker

As a dog walker, you'll walk and care for pets. You have to make sure the dogs get enough exercise, are walked safely to and from their homes, and have access to food and water. The National average salary for this is $15.23 per hour.

3) Tutor

Tutors work with students one-on-one to assist them in improving their knowledge in specific disciplines. They will frequently work with a student who is having difficulty in a particular class to help explain complex issues in layman's terms.

4) Freelancer

Freelancing is a way to supplement your income by utilizing talents. Many firms do not want to commit to adding an employee to their payroll, and freelance job options abound. You have complete freedom to work as much or as little as you wish. If you're not sure what you could accomplish, look through the job listings on Upwork or Outsourcely. According to Upwork's Freelancing in America report, professional freelancers earn a median hourly rate of $28, accounting for more than 70% of all employees in the United States.

Online

1) Ad watcher

You heard it right! Sites such as Inbox Dollars will pay you to perform chores such as watching advertisements. It's a cool way to get paid since watching ads is something you already do each day.

2) Brand ambassador

Brand ambassadors are always needed to introduce new clients to their website. Boostapal Ambassador Program is one such brand, and they will pay you $10 for each new student you enroll.

3) Online writer

Writing articles for websites and blogs is a way to earn money. For writing samples, you can take papers you've written in school and pitch them to sites that hire teenagers. There are sites that periodically pay teen writers, and there are those like

Hubpages, which accepts teen writers under the age of 18 as long as they have parental permission.

Working part-time while in school can be a wonderful way to supplement your income. You'll meet new people, gain valuable life skills, and improve your résumé in preparation for applying for your ideal job! Earning your own money is one of the most obvious benefits you can have if you work part-time. This will make you feel independent and empowered. So, it is a good idea to find a part-time job now that you are young and have lots to learn.

Starting your own business

Age is nothing but a number. This adage has been successfully proven by older people who have overcome challenges and became success stories. But can this be done the other way around?

The following successful people who started at a young age in dabbling with entrepreneurship have shown that young people can make it big early in their lifetimes.

We cannot begin this discussion with someone other than Mark Zuckerberg. Facebook is a testament to the man's achievement, as he founded it when he was only 19 years old.

Within a few years of its introduction, Facebook has established itself as one of the most widely utilized social networking platforms on the planet. Facebook is still growing and employing thousands of people today. Zuckerberg, an inspiration to numerous individuals, is currently valued at $43 billion USD and continues to grow as an entrepreneur.

He was only 19 years old when Blake Ross launched his baby - Mozilla Firefox. At a period when most people used their operating system's default browser or Google Chrome, Firefox built a loyal following of users. Firefox is now one of the most popular web browsers on a variety of systems, including Windows, Linux, and Android.

Catherine Cook, together with her brother Dave, came up with the idea of digitizing high school yearbooks and posting them online at the age of 15. When individuals are learning how to write a proper essay for their college applications, the sibling tandem launched MyYearbook.com with the help of their eldest brother, Geoff Cook. In the early days of the MyYearbook, Catherine and Dave were among the youngest billionaires.

Other examples of entrepreneurs at a tender age are these teens who were dubbed "Top 10 Teen Entrepreneurs To Watch In 2020" in an article by Grey Journal.

Cory Nieves - 16

Mr. Cory's Cookies is his company, and he is the founder and CEO. Nieves' entrepreneurial adventure began at a young age, with one of his first endeavors being the sale of Swiss Miss for $1 per cup. When he was a bit younger, he saw an opportunity and began looking for the ultimate cookie recipe. He and his mother soon began taking their cookies with them wherever they went. The company now offers over 14 different varieties.

John Feinsibler - 17

He is the founder of Gimkit, a learning application allowing teachers to create kits to be used in classes. These kits are quizzes that let students put what they've learned in class to the test. When John was brainstorming for a new startup, he stumbled across Kahoot, a similar tool to Gimkit, and wanted to improve it.

Rachel Zietz - 18

Gladiator Lacrosse, founded by Rachel Zietz, is a lacrosse equipment manufacturer that focuses on high-quality, long-lasting equipment at affordable rates. Rachel had already developed a $1 million corporation by the age of 15. She was also a finalist for the Greater Miami Chamber of Commerce's 2015 Entrepreneur Award and appeared on Shark Tank.

All successful entrepreneurs begin their careers when they are young. Above and beyond all of the advantages of starting your own business, the genuine value it provides cannot be measured in dollars or magazine features. Its genuine merit, especially when you're a teenager, is simply in the lessons you acquire from experience.

So, how do you start your own business?

First, you should make a business plan.

A business plan is highly useful in laying out how the company will operate. Make sure to factor in the expenditures of running the company so that unanticipated expenses are kept to a minimum. Having a strategy in place aids in keeping the company on track.

Unless there is a business design in place, it is simple for youngsters to stray off and deviate from the initial plan. Here are some pointers to help you flesh out your concepts and lay a foundation for your business plan.

Brainstorm Ideas.

You'll need ideas to launch any business plan. Try to write down all the potential business concepts. What is your interest? Do you have a knack for social media or enjoy programming on the computer? Is a seasonal business, such as snow shoveling or grass mowing, a better fit? Are you good at arts and crafts like knitting or painting?

The next step is to determine whether the idea is a product or a service. Maybe you like to paint, you can sell your paintings at a local craft fair or on the internet. Or perhaps you could help a local business with its social media. Select an idea that resonates with you the best.

Set out goals and objectives.

It's now time to jot down the business's goals and objectives. Every business owner should be well-versed in all aspects of his or her business. For example, a goal of a social media marketing company might be to give affordable, straightforward campaigns to local businesses.

Add up the numbers.

Calculating expenses to estimate how much you need to charge to earn a profit is a crucial aspect of any business plan.

Second, you would be smart to name your business.

Keep in mind that your company's name will provide your customers with a first impression. The name should embody the practical use of your products or services for your customers, signify your differentiation from competitors- how you'll stand out from others, and reflect your business's philosophy.

Consider a variety of names for your product or service, keeping in mind that the more your name conveys about your company to people, the less work you'll have to put in to describe it. Once you've decided on a name, check to see whether it's already been taken by another company or product.

Lastly, you'll want to market your business.

Determine who you want to reach. Figuring out who can benefit the most from your product or service is crucial to the growth of your business. The more you know about your customers, the faster your company will grow.

Another important step in guaranteeing the success of your venture is to get the word out about it. Thanks to the internet, it is now easier than ever to sell your product or service.

Create a website for your company first. There are numerous free and simple-to-use websites available, such as WordPress or Tumblr. To get the word out, use social media sites like Facebook, Twitter, Instagram, or Tiktok. It's practically free promotion, and it's a fantastic method to get the word out quickly.

Create a business card that includes a few key details about your business, such as your website and contact information. Reach out to local businesses. Request permission to display a flyer with your contact information so that others in the community can get in touch with you.

Possible downsides of working as a teen

It would help to know what can be affected if you do have your business during your teen years.

Less time to study.

Students who work more than 20 hours per week had worse grade point averages than students who work 10 hours or less per week, according to research. When you are employed, you may have to stay up late to finish your schoolwork, or you may put less effort into school.

Negative work impression.

Working for an unorganized employer or an untrained boss may give you a negative opinion of work. Unfortunately, statistics suggest that when teenagers start working, they are more likely to be sexually harassed.

Missed opportunities.

Having to work a shift may detract from the high school experience. If you work part-time, it may be tough for you to participate in a school sports team, drama production, or volunteer activity.

More stress.

If a teen works too many hours, he or she may feel anxious. A job's objective is to provide you with a little more independence by allowing you to earn your own money. What good is it if you never have time to spend that money having fun?

One other issue with teenagers working is that they are generally inexperienced and naive, making them vulnerable to unfair treatment and exploitation by employers. While your experience level may make it appear that you have restricted freedom at work, you are legally entitled to individual rights as an employee. Here are some of them, beginning with your most fundamental rights as an employee.

Regardless of age, you're entitled to several essential rights as an employee. These include, among other things, the right to privacy and just compensation. You should have your workspace and have access to all permissible revenue, including overtime, as an employee. Privacy rights apply to your personal belongings, any storage lockers, and any private mail addressed to you in most states.

You can also have privacy rights when it comes to phone calls or voicemail messages. Although businesses utilize electronic surveillance to monitor phone calls and voicemails, the Electronic Communications Privacy Act places legal restrictions on this practice. As a result, employers who read, delete, disclose, or prohibit access to voicemail messages may be subject to legal action.

If you're under the age of 20, the Fair Labor Standards Act allows you to be paid as little as $4.25 per hour for the first 90 days of your job. Only after you reach the age of 20 will you be eligible for the $7.25 minimum wage. Please note that rates vary by state.

If you're under the age of 16, federal law limits the amount of time you can work. You are not permitted to work during school hours or for more than three hours on a school day. When school is not in session, you cannot work more than eight hours per day or more than 40 hours per week.

Is all this a lot to take in? I understand, but if you're eager to get out and work, you must understand your rights and entitlements. Make the most of your opportunity while protecting yourself.

Job Tips

Now for some tips:

1. Be on time! Accountability and punctuality are the foundations of teen work etiquette.

2. Always look presentable. The way you dress at work affects how managers, coworkers, and customers see you.

3. Speak clearly. The majority of jobs require good verbal communication abilities. You'll have to communicate with your employer, coworkers, and customers.

4. Listen. Excellent listening skills will be necessary regardless of what occupation you wish to pursue in the future. They enable you to carry out your boss's orders and respond to client inquiries.

5. Be considerate. Your employer may require you to deal with customers in some way. When you're doing so, always keep the customer's best interest in mind.

6. Accept constructive feedback and learn from your mistakes. It's quite acceptable to make mistakes when you're learning something new.

Understand your paycheck

It's a fantastic feeling to receive your first paycheck! It's important to read your pay stub and look for any mistakes. Income tax and employee benefit programs can appear to be complex. Looking at each thing in terms of dollars and cents can be helpful.

Don't be startled if your pay doesn't match the equation of hours worked, or if your check isn't for the amount you expected.

Here are some of the things you should know to understand your paycheck better:

1) Gross pay is calculated as follows:

If you're paid $15 per hour and work 20 hours per week, your gross compensation will be $300.

Your gross compensation is the number you'll need to provide on rental applications, mortgage applications, and other documents.

2) Your net income is your take-home pay. It's lower than the gross pay because taxes, health benefits, fees, and others are deducted.
3) Mandatory deductions are deducted automatically from your gross pay. When your annual earnings exceed $7,600, you must start paying federal income tax. All workers are required to contribute to Social Security and Medicare. FICA, a payroll tax, funds both programs.

You'll want to double-check that your pay stub's wage and hours worked are right. Talk to your human resources person if you see any issues. They'll be able to assist you in deciphering what you're seeing—and, if necessary, rectify mistakes.

Mandatory payroll deductions

1) FICA

Social Security and Medicare taxes make up the Federal Insurance Contributions Act (FICA). FICA tax is paid equally by both the employee and the employer. If an employee's salary is at or below the Social Security pay base, the Social Security tax is 6.2 percent. The Medicare tax is 1.45% of the employee's taxable wages under Medicare. The overall FICA deduction from an employee's paycheck is 7.65 percent. You must also pay a 7.65% payment as the employer.

2) Federal income tax

This is calculated based on your Form W-4 information and your gross pay. To compute the amount withheld from your paycheck, the Payroll team utilizes the IRS's Publication 15-T's income tax withholding tables. Transportation, education, and the military are all supported by federal income taxes.

3) State and local taxes

Each state has its unique system of income taxation. Check with your state to see how much you need to withhold from an employee's paycheck for state and local taxes. If you're a new employer, check out our state-by-state guide to payroll information. State and municipal taxes, like federal taxes, fund public services.

4) Wage garnishments

These deductions are necessary if one of your employees has an unpaid debt. If you need to withhold garnishments from an employee's paycheck, you will receive an order from a court or government agency with more information.

Voluntary payroll deductions

1) Health insurance premiums

These deductions vary depending on what plan you choose. Doctor visits and medicines are covered by health insurance.

2) Retirement plans

You may want to have money deducted from your paycheck for a personal retirement fund. An IRA (Individual Retirement Account) or a 401(k) are two examples of small company retirement plans.

3) Life insurance premiums

You can choose to have money deducted from your paycheck to pay for life insurance premiums. This would cover payment for beneficiaries.

Taxes

The government collects taxes so that they can raise revenue to fund the country's activities. It is the most feasible way for the officials to fund expenditures on public goods and services that you, as a citizen, need.

Do you need to pay income tax? Yes. If your earned income exceeds $12,550 (rising to $12,950 in 2022), you must submit taxes. Please note that you can pay self-employment tax as an independent contractor by completing a Schedule SE with your tax return.

Unearned income that belongs to a child is subject to kiddie tax rules. If your child earns more than $2,200 in unearned income, some of it will be taxed at estate and trust tax rates (for tax years 2018 and 2019) or at the parent's highest marginal tax rate (beginning in 2020).

Why file a tax return even if it's not required? Here are reasons why it's an advantage for you to file a tax return:

1) You can use it as a legal document.

The filed return can serve as proof of identification (and even proof of address) which you can use when you apply for documents such as Financial Aid (FAFSA)

2) You can use it to claim deductions.

The government offers some deductions to you in order to ease the load on taxpayers and encourage more individuals to pay their taxes. However, you must file an income tax return to be eligible for these tax benefits. You cannot claim deductions if you have not submitted an ITR.

3) You can use it to file for a loan

When applying for a loan, the bank will ask you to submit certain paperwork. One key document requested is evidence of income. Income Tax Returns (ITRs) for the previous three years were commonly requested by banks. This is done to determine if you will be able to repay the loan based on your history and current financial condition.

4) You can use it when you go abroad.

Some countries require ITR forms. You have an increased chances of receiving a visa if you have a history of filing income tax returns.

What do you need to file an income tax return?

Here's a checklist:

1) Personal Information, such as your name (as shown in your Social Security card), date of birth, Social Security number, a copy of the previous year's federal and state tax returns, and bank information.
2) Source of Income

You need a form documenting the income you received for the last year. An example would be W-2s that would be provided by your employer.

3) Self-Employment and Business Records

If you are self-employed, you must disclose your earnings. You can also deduct business expenses from your gross income to reduce your taxable income.

4) Deductions

Exemptions can help you lower your taxable income and increase your refund by lowering the amount of tax you owe. You can either take the standard deduction (a fixed amount dependent on your filing status) or itemize deductions.

5) Tax Credits

These are reductions in the amount of tax you owe on a dollar-for-dollar basis.

6) Expected Tax Payments

If you're self-employed or earn a lot of money and don't have federal and state income tax withheld, you may have to make estimated tax payments. Make sure you include those estimates on your tax return to avoid paying twice.

It may take some time to gather all of this information before filing your return, but it will ensure that you have everything you need to claim every tax deduction and credit available to you.

Next Steps

You have been given several money-making options. Which looks interesting to you? One thing you need to remember is to choose something you are good at or enjoy doing.

You can pick three to five from the above selections. You can research them further so you have ample details for a better understanding. Then, you can begin job hunting!

Chapter two has given you many tips and details that can serve as a good foundation as you make your mark in the employment world.

Starting a business or working part-time at a young age has a number of outcomes for your life. It teaches you many things that you wouldn't learn in school. Having a job or owning a business can provide you with a sense of satisfaction and personal achievement.

Having a job or owning a business also gives you a much broader view of life, and meeting with people you might not otherwise meet is a terrific way to broaden your horizons. Having these opportunities will help you pave the way to adulthood.

Making your own money is a satisfying, empowering, and liberating experience, I tell you. For me, it was even a humbling experience.

When you get a job, you will not only have some money, but you will also have some experience. Networking and skill development are also two of the most important elements you'll gain when you have a job.

Imagine now that you are being handed out your paycheck - what are you going to do with it? How will you spend it?

Chapter Three

Creating Your First Budget

Importance of saving your money

When you start earning your own money, it's easy to want to spend it on things your parents can't or won't buy for you. However, it's critical to set aside a portion, if not the entirety, of your paycheck when it arrives.

Not enough details to convince you yet? Maybe these reasons would do the trick:

1) Saving money means you have an emergency fund.

Emergency funds may be alien to you at this point. You typically associate this with your parents or the "grown-ups." But you need such a fund too! Remember that as a teen, your lifestyle has changed, and your responsibilities have grown.

You might need an emergency fund for: car repairs, phone data charges, and the like.

You can only get out of these situations if you have saved some of your allowance or hard-earned money.

2) Saving money means you can buy stuff that your parents don't want to buy for you.

You have to accept the fact that your parents might not be willing to buy you some stuff for you anymore. After all, you are on your way to becoming an adult. So, certain privileges are removed.

But you don't have to worry because you can buy yourself those things that you want if you learn how to save. Also, some of the buying responsibilities being turned over to you will help you in the long run. Having money responsibilities at an early age ensures that you are not thrown into the deep end when you get your first apartment. You also will not have the shock of your life by surmounting bills.

3) Saving money can help you develop sensible spending and discipline.

Along with planning, a healthy savings habit teaches you discipline, which you can apply to other aspects of your life. The practice of reinforcing a habit over time causes it to endure a lifetime. It may be easier to distinguish between wants and needs if you have a disciplined attitude toward money.

Because money is finite and your needs often outnumber your ability to pay, saving teaches you to consider trade-offs and opportunity costs, which can lead to better spending decisions. You may learn to avoid impulse purchases and become a better judge of whether something is a good buy.

4) Saving money can teach you to create money goals.

Saving money requires you to create financial goals and consider what you want to do with your savings in the future. While it may be easy for you to focus on your current lifestyle, taking control of some of your own spending and saving goals, with a timeframe in mind would demonstrate that you comprehend your money or wealth in the long run.

What you can do is make a list of your financial priorities. Make a reasonable strategy and encourage yourself to follow it.

5) Saving money gives you more control.

I'm sure at this point in your life, you want to exert some control over your life. All your life, you have been hiding behind your parents' shadow, allowing them to make decisions for you. Now, by saving money, you can have that longed-for autonomy.

What do you want to have control of?

What to wear...

What to eat...

What to drink...

What to watch...

Saving gives you the freedom to choose. You have more control over your finances if you save money.

6) Saving money opens up a whole set of opportunities.

Go on a trip.

Throw a party.

Buy a car.

Take extra lessons.

Pay for room renovation.

It can be a bummer when certain wants are not fulfilled. It can be disheartening when you want to throw yourself a sweet sixteen party, but your parents are on a tight budget. You want to join your friends for an out-of-town trip, but you don't have extra funds.

That's when your savings would come in handy.

7) Saving money allows you to help others or make others happy.

Your parents might be a little short on cash. You can step in and lend them some money.

You can make some donations to charity. You can buy your sibling something nice for their birthday. You can treat your grandparents to a nice meal.

There are many ways for you to render help. Your saved money can go a long way.

Guys, you need to know that proactive money management is always better than reactive money management.

Proactive money management is taking steps and making decisions today with the goal of improving your financial situation in the future. It's about anticipating potential financial difficulties rather than waiting for them to occur before taking action.

Waiting for financial crises to strike before acting, making decisions with no actual plan, and resources restricted to what you can scrape together right now is referred to as reactive money management. If you are reactive, the following can happen, and you might not be able to cope:

Not having sufficient money to go to college

When this happens, and there are scholarships or grants available, you are forced to take out student loans, which you will learn later on can take a toll on your finances once you work.

Falling behind in paying your bills

You don't want this to happen. Getting cut from your phone plan is a hassle. And think about the inconvenience if utilities are not paid on time.

Not being able to pay for car repairs

Having your own car is not a luxury. It's a necessity. So, not having saved money for emergency repairs would inconvenience you a lot.

Start saving now; prepare yourself for the future.

What are you saving for?

What it will be used for is one of the most thrilling aspects of the process of saving money. You get to consider what those savings will be worth in the long run, how you can use them in advance, and how to get the most out of your money.

With all these thoughts, you can begin to create your financial goals.

What are financial goals? Long-term, short-term, and intermediate financial goals are the building blocks of a comprehensive financial strategy. The finest financial goals are those that are in line with your personal beliefs and ambitions.

No, don't mistake goals for a budget or financial plan. Financial goals are measurable milestones that, when achieved, get you closer to your ideal future.

Why do you need to set financial goals for yourself?

Generally, setting financial objectives is critical to achieving financial success. After you've set these objectives, you may write and follow a plan to achieve them. It keeps you focused and assures you that you're on the correct track.

Now, let's check some of the best reasons why you should set some financial goals for your future.

These goals give you a sense of direction.

What do you hope to achieve? How can you measure your success?

You can have clear-cut answers to these questions if you set financial goals. You'll know what your end goal is and what you need to do to get there once you have your answers, which will be unique to you and your personal and professional situations.

Goals necessitate a realistic plan.

Establishing goals requires you to create a specific and realistic plan so that there are steps to follow in order. And when the steps are outlined, the required courses of action will follow.

Your plan needs dedication. As a result, you develop a sense of urgency. The "I must do this" attitude is born, increasing your chances of success.

Setting financial goals determine the amount of money you'll need to save.

How much money do you need to save and invest in order to achieve your financial objectives? Again, your goals can answer such a question. You have the opportunity to quantify or put a number on your ambitions.

Whatever amount you identify, you may track your progress toward it and make changes as necessary to expedite things. It makes budgeting a whole lot easier.

These goals allow you to create different strategies in order for you to achieve them.

Your financial objectives will determine the techniques you'll need to reach them. If your financial goals are small, saving may be sufficient.

If you have more ambitious financial objectives, such as buying a house, retiring early, or taking a year off to travel, you may need to combine a number of tactics to improve your income, cut expenses, and invest your savings in stocks or shares to grow your money faster.

What this all means is that you are able to design your path. These strategies help you pick out the stones that litter your path to success.

These aims shape your career decisions.

With the help of these goals, you can make better job decisions. If you have clear ambitions, you'll need to consider how much time you can afford to take off, what you'll need to do to gain a promotion or a raise, and so on.

Some situations may require you to leave the comfort of a 9-to-5 job and start your own business, which, while hazardous, can be more lucrative in the long run. Your career planning and financial planning can complement each other once you know what your financial goals are.

You maintain your focus when you have clear-cut financial goals.

Setting financial goals will help you keep your mind on the prize. It's well worth taking a picture of one or more of your goals – be it a house or a car or a job you can do from the beach – and sticking it up on the wall by your desk.

This will help you stick to your guns when you're tempted to splurge on something you don't need and remind you why you're working extra hours. In this case, the end will justify the means, and that will help you stay on track.

You'll be able to find the right tools to assist you.

When you have outlined what you want to accomplish, you can begin to employ the necessary and applicable tools.

There are many tools available to assist you in saving, earning more money, and investing your money. Many of these apps are free to download from the Apple App Store or Google Play Store, but some require a subscription or a cost to obtain.

For example, you may start investing using the Acorns app, save automatically with Plum, and track your money with Cleo.

Setting financial goals will allow you to critically examine which tools will assist you on your journey, allowing you to purchase just those that will be most beneficial to you.

It's pointless to waste money on useless items; instead, put your money on the things that will benefit you the most.

You gain a sense of accomplishment.

It can take a long time to achieve your financial objectives. But laying them out requires both thought and discipline. Writing things down is an accomplishment in and of itself, so pat yourself on the back after you've finished.

Give yourself a pat on the back also for getting started on your new financial path and overcoming the first hurdle. Setting the objectives is the first step toward achieving them.

Now, why don't you pick up a pen and paper and start writing those goals?!

Setting your own financial goals

Do you have a pen and paper handy? Yes, you can go ahead and write it all down. Then, in your car, on your desk, or on your bathroom mirror, stick them. Put them in your phone's Notes app, take a screenshot, then set it as your wallpaper so you can view them all the time! Keeping your goals visible will help you stay on track.

How do you start?

First, think of both short-term and long-term goals. When you set a long-term goal, you must now maintain your attention until you reach your final goal. As a result, in addition to a long-term objective, you'll need a lot of short-term goals to stay on course and avoid becoming lost.

Long-term objectives are those you establish for yourself for the distant future, while short-term goals are ones you set for the near future. Long-term objectives are impossible to achieve in a span of hours, days, and weeks. It typically takes 3 months to save up for a long-term goal. Meanwhile, for the short-term, it can take more than one pay cycle, but less than one month to save up for.

Years of dedication, hard work, and planning are required. Imagining what you want to accomplish in the future might be thrilling, but putting the plan into action can be difficult. As a result, you set multiple short-term goals in order to develop an effective approach to achieving your long-term objectives.

Second, consider your future. When you were little, how did you imagine life would be when you became a teen? Now that you are one, can you see any similarities to what you imagined?

Part of setting financial goals is imagining your future. Visualizing your future is essential because it focuses your attention on it right now. Knowing who you want to be, how you want to act, and the life you want to live allows you to act in a way that will lead you to that ideal vision.

Ten years from now, do you envision yourself with a family? Do you see how many kids you have? With these details, it's easy for you to work out your financial goals since you would consider how your family life would be affected by the goals you set.

To have successful financial goals, it must be YOUR goals. You may be prone to agreeing to what your parents desire for you at your age. Don't let someone else dictate your goals, no matter how good their intentions are. Everything must stem from what you want your life to be.

Of course, I'm not saying to disregard what your parents say. Their experience and wisdom could help you a lot. But never allow their views to overtake yours.

Have you heard of SMART goals?

SMART is an acronym composed of the following meanings:

S- Specific

M- Measurable

A - Achievable

R - Relevant

T - Time-Bound

SMART GOALS

These criteria are attributed to Peter Drucker's Management by Objectives concept.

What does Specific mean?

Your goal should be clear and specific so that you can focus your efforts and feel genuinely motivated to achieve it. When writing your goal, try to answer the five "W" questions: What, Why, Who, Where, and Which.

Now, let's look at Measurable.

It's critical to set measurable goals so you can keep track of your progress and stay motivated. Evaluating progress allows you to meet deadlines, stay focused, and experience the excitement of getting closer to your goal.

Typically, this part answers questions.

Achievable is next.

To be successful, your goal must also be realistic and attainable. In other words, it should be challenging while remaining doable. When you set an attainable goal, you can discover previously unnoticed resources and opportunities that can help you get closer to it.

The "how" questions are also applicable here.

Let's go to Relevant.

Relevancy ensures that your goal is important to you and is also aligned with other relevant goals. We all need help and support to achieve our goals, but it's critical to maintain control over them. As a result, make sure that your plans propel everyone forward while still holding you accountable for achieving your own goals.

Usually, questions applicable are those answerable by yes or no.

Lastly, we have Time-Bound.

You need target dates for your goals. Having a deadline to work toward and something to focus on gives you focus. This area of the SMART goal technique helps prevent everyday tasks from prioritizing your longer-term goals.

You can consider when and what questions here.

Looking at all these details, what SMART financial goals can you create?

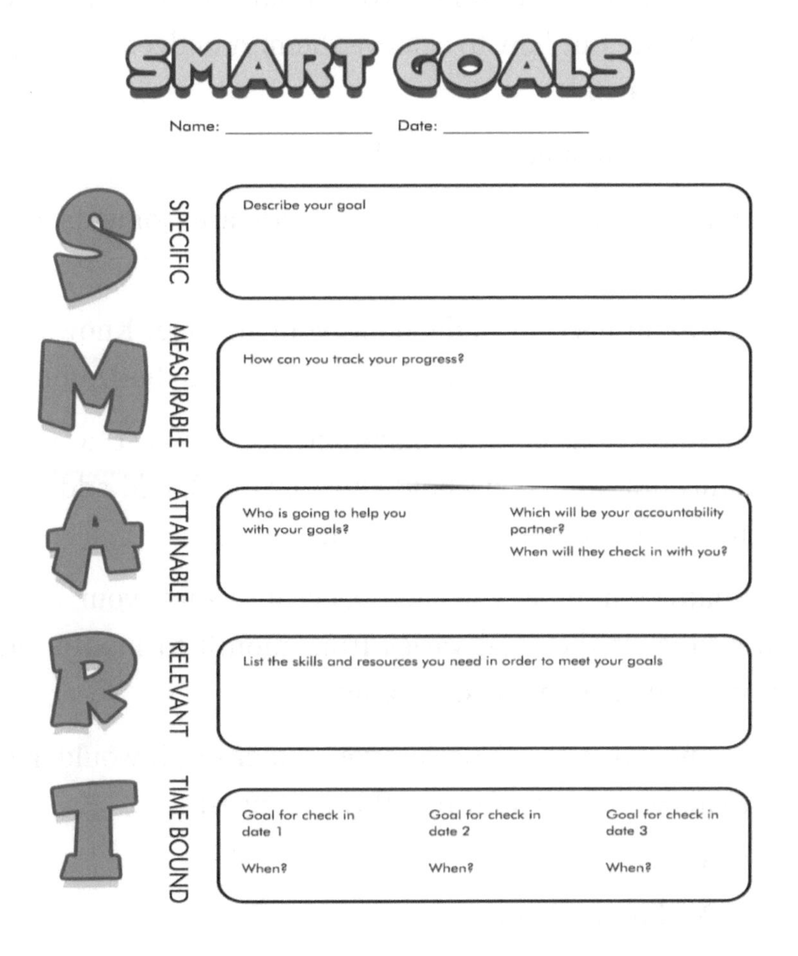

Your budget

Why do you need to budget?

While geography, math, history, and other subjects are required for a high school diploma, some vital life skills are not always taught in school. Budgeting is a practical skill that you can use every day to help you achieve financial success.

Once you've determined your financial objectives, you'll need to figure out how to achieve them. A budget can help you in that endeavor.

How do you make a budget?

Budgeting is not that easy. There are some factors to consider.

First, you need to understand your income. Knowing how much money you make is an important step in budgeting.

Whether you have a part-time job or just a monthly allowance for your household chores, you should add up how much money you make each month.

Whatever number you choose, use it to guide your spending and saving. If the total varies from month to month, err on caution and stick to the lower amount.

Second, you need to project your expenses. It would help for you to make a list of your monthly expenses:

- Utility bills
- Phone charges
- Transportation
- School supplies
- Car insurance
- Gas
- Snacks
- Other fees

Even if you only have an allowance, you can still project your expenses. Having an estimate of your expenses allows you to create a more efficient budget plan.

Third, you can come up with budget categories. When creating categories, keep two main ones in mind: saving (savings account, college expenses, trip) and spending (phone bill, food, gas).

Fourth, you can select a budgeting strategy. Once you've identified all of your categories, it's time to determine how much money to allot to each one. You can accomplish this through a variety of budgeting methods.

The 50/30/20

You can allocate your money in the following percentages: 50% for necessary expenses, 30% for want expenses, and 20% for savings.

Zero-based budgeting

HOW TO CREATE A ZERO-BASED BUDGET	
Total Monthly Income: $3,250	
Rent	$1,200
Utilities	$120
Groceries	$400
Phone bill	$80
Gas	$250
Insurance	$100
Clothes	$100
Entertainment	$150
Charity	$100
Travel Fund	$100
Emergency Fund	$150
Retirement	$200
Loans	$200
Misc.	$100
Amount Left Over: $0	

This method is based on the idea that the result is zero when your expenses are subtracted from your income. Estimate the cost of each budget category and divide your income until it reaches zero, using your estimates as a guide.

Pay yourself first method

Paying yourself first means putting a certain amount or percentage of your income into savings. Whatever money remains is yours to spend however you see fit.

Did you know that there are budget apps you can use? Look these up and download which you think is the best one to keep track of your budget.

- Mint
- Toshl Finance
- Left to Spend
- Smarty Pig

Revisit your budget every quarter or every year. You need to update or improve on it because your situation and needs change as you grow older.

You have to be realistic when budgeting and the plan must be simple enough so you can stick to it.

Don't deprive yourself. Make sure to include some fun in your budget.

Before I end this chapter, here are some budgeting tips for you:

- Keep your end goal in mind.
- Seek your parents' advice.

As I said, they have the experience. If you feel uncomfortable talking to your parents about money, you can reach out to other experienced family members or budget experts. You can also watch budget advice through social media.

- Save first; spend later. Treat savings like an expense.
- Keep track of how much money you receive and how much money you spend.
- Learn from your mistakes.

Next Steps

Now that you have all this information, it's high time for you to start thinking about what you intend to use your money for. Don't sell yourself short. It's always great to have short- and long-term goals.

As you are reading this, what thoughts come to mind about your future? Are you the type of person who desires an elaborate wedding? Do you want to take your parents on an ideal out-of-the-country vacation? Do you want to own some properties?

I encourage you to put all these thoughts onto paper. Make a vision board. With these objectives in mind, you can begin preparing your budget.

Chapter three showed you that budgeting is one of the most important things you can do to gain financial control and improve your future. Most people don't start budgeting until they're much older. And some only do once they've run into financial difficulties.

Spending money comes naturally for everyone. But as a teen, you may tend to overspend if you don't become aware of how important budgeting is.

Your parents may teach you, and or you may have read some books about handling money. But you need to hone those skills.

Budgeting as a teen can give you a significant head start on saving and reaching your financial goals. Not to mention, by the time you reach adulthood, you'll be comfortable managing your finances.

Chapter Four

Opening Your First Bank Account

When you were a kid, a piggy bank could have sufficed, but once you start earning and growing money, it's no longer sufficient. Banking will become a need for any young adult who wishes to learn to drive for the first time or who wishes to begin their education path.

There's a lot about banking that you don't learn in school. I hope what I'm about to share will help you get started.

Putting Money in the Bank

It is preferable to keep money in the bank rather than at home. For starters, banks have insurance that helps you recover your funds in the event of unauthorized withdrawals or charges. Furthermore, by storing your money in the bank, you will be able to earn interest, which is not feasible when you store it at home.

If you're still questioning if it is a good idea, here are some of the reasons why you should keep your money in the bank:

1) Your savings can earn interest.

One of the most compelling reasons to keep your money in the bank rather than at home is the opportunity to earn interest. If you don't earn interest, you'll be losing money every year due to inflation. I don't know about you, but if I'm going to save money, I'd like it to have some worth.

To be clear, simply depositing money in a bank does not guarantee that you will receive interest. Alternatively, even if you receive interest, many bank accounts do not generate enough to keep up with inflation. So, when you want to open a savings account, make sure it earns between 1% and 2% per year.

2) Your money is insured.

Another important reason to keep your money in the bank rather than at home is that banks carry insurance that will cover you if any part of your money is stolen. You would not be accountable for anything if someone obtained access to your checking or savings account and withdrew or spent your money, and you would receive a full refund.

On the other hand, would you be able to recoup the money you kept at home if it was stolen? I assume that the money would vanish permanently. Simply said, if you want your hard-earned money to be safe, put it in the bank.

3) Your money is easily accessible.

While having money in a savings account isn't as convenient as having cash in your sock drawer, your financial resources are still excellent and available. So, if you ever need money for an emergency or an unforeseen bill, you won't have any trouble getting it.

You can do online banking. Do you need to send money to someone? E-transfer is a simple way to accomplish this. Do you have monthly bills to pay? Yes, you can pay your bills online using online banking. Do you need to pay off your Visa? The answer? Online banking.

I could go on and on, but the point is that when you open an account with a bank, you gain access to their online banking interface, which will save you time and effort.

4) A paycheck goes directly through bank accounts. Many employers prefer to send their employee's paychecks to the bank rather than giving them cash or a payroll check. It is much more convenient, and there won't be any risk that your paychecks will get lost or stolen.

And it's not all about the money. Having a savings account can teach you other things:

1) Independence

Teenagers are trusted to manage their own money when creating a personal checking or savings account. When a person earns their own money, they are more aware of how it leaves their account. The capacity to budget, and get insights into where they might cut back on spending can lead to a firm awareness that their financial future is closely tied to their current decisions.

2) Good Habits

Early on, you may learn to save and investigate investments. You can plan for retirement by instilling excellent savings habits.

Teens who can earn self-incentives, such as knowing that putting 15% into savings leads to 15% for pleasure spending later, will develop excellent savings and spending habits.

3) Financial Literacy

You can learn to make your money work in addition to the convenience of automatic bill payments. Whether it's a certificate of deposit (CD) or another account, such as a money market deposit account, you will strengthen your banking relationship with the institution that will accompany you on your journey to financial literacy.

You will be able to control your financial future if you are financially literate. Building a solid financial foundation and the financial literacy that goes with it can have a huge payoff.

4) Access to services

To begin, you can use some of the services your bank provides. Credit unions are a great way to connect with a financial advisor, and they also provide vehicle and housing loans, budgeting essentials, debt consolidation, and financial education.

If your parents have not made you have one yet, you should seriously think of opening a savings account. Having a teen savings account is one of the first steps in securing a solid financial future with long-term rewards.

Different bank accounts

It's good to invest in the best account type for your financial goals. Different types of bank accounts are designed to meet particular needs, ensuring that you have the necessary tools for spending and saving. A bank account helps you maximize your bank's return, save fees, and manage your money more efficiently.

Check out this list:

1) Savings Account.

A first bank account for children or teenagers and an account for adults wishing to earn interest on savings or keep funds they might otherwise spend. Your relationship with a financial institution begins when you open a savings account.

When you join a credit union, for example, your "share" or savings account creates your membership.

2) Checking Account.

Everyday spending is done with checking accounts. A linked debit card that you may use for purchases or ATM withdrawals and check-writing capabilities are the main characteristics of this sort of bank account. You can deposit cash or checks as well as pay bills with this account type. Most banks now offer online bill-paying through checking accounts, making payments more convenient.

While standard checking accounts do not pay interest, interest-bearing checking accounts allow you to earn additional income on top of your savings account's interest. This basic bank account is ideal for storing funds for short-term use and is crucial for monitoring your monthly financial flow.

3) Money Market Accounts.

This type of account is for people with high balances in their account that want to earn higher interest rates. Money market accounts demand a more outstanding minimum balance than other types of bank accounts.

4) Certificate of Deposit.

This type is similar to a savings account that stores your money for a set period, three months or five years. To avoid an early withdrawal penalty, you must agree to keep your money in the CD for the entire period (ending on the "maturity date"). You'll have to pay the penalty if you opt to withdraw your funds early. That penalty might wipe out all of your earnings and possibly deplete your initial deposit.

5) Retirement Accounts.

As the name implies, these are accounts that you utilize to save money for retirement spending. Individual retirement accounts (IRAs) are available at most banks, but some offer 401(k) and other retirement accounts for small enterprises. Tax advantages are available in almost all types of retirement funds.

You can avoid paying income tax on the growth of your contributions in both IRAs and 401(k) plans, but you'll have to pay taxes at different times, depending on the account type. Traditional IRA and 401(k) contributions lower your taxes now, but withdrawals will be taxed later. Contributions to a Roth IRA don't save you money right now, but you won't have to pay taxes on withdrawals later.

These are the most satisfactory bank accounts for saving for the future because they allow you to put your money in investments, earning higher returns than you would on other bank accounts.

Let me guess. You want to know which account makes the most money, right?

If your bank offers a regular IRA or a similar retirement account with a mix of equities and bonds, that is your greatest long-term savings option. High-yield savings accounts and money market ones will outperform standard savings and checking accounts in the short-term development.

You can also set up one type of bank account for yourself. Your financial condition and aspirations will determine how many separate accounts you require. It's a good idea to strive toward having a savings account, a checking account, and a retirement account at the very least. After you've got those three, you can look into other accounts that could provide short- or long-term development.

How to open your first bank account

How to Open a Bank Account

Step 1 Collect Documents	Step 2 Choose a Bank or Credit Union	Step 3 Apply and Fund Your Account
Identification	Bank	Cash
Proof of Address	Credit Union	Check
Social Security Number	Online Bank	Wire Transfer

I can still recall the day I opened my first bank account. It's like my maturity has gone to a whole new level. I felt so adult!

But somehow, I wished someone could have told me some tips about it during that time. I could have used the advice so that some questionable decisions could have been prevented.

That's why I want you guys to know all there is to know in this book. I want to prepare you for something as big as your first bank account.

Personal finance is frequently absent from school curricula, even though it is an important subject. Teens like yourself need to gain real-world financial experience. Learning how to utilize real money in your bank accounts is one approach to do so.

So how do you open an account?

Hold on. You cannot march yourself up to the bank counter and immediately have an account under your name. Getting a bank account when you're under the age of 18 has some regulations.

Although only an adult, generally a parent, grandparent, or guardian, can open a savings account for a minor, the name of the adolescent must be included in the account and records. It's that simple.

Both names remain on the bank account for as long as it is open when it is a joint account. However, once you have legally become an adult, the parent's name can be removed from the account.

What savings account is applicable for teens? A standard or basic savings account is open to anyone.

You can use bank accounts specifically for children or minors. There are several names for these types of savings accounts:

- Teen savings account
- Youth savings account
- Student savings account

What are the requirements needed? You need to be aware so that you can make the necessary preparations.

You need a valid photo ID issued by the government, such as a driver's license or passport. Non-drivers can obtain a state identification card from the Department of Motor Vehicles.

Other basic information, such as your date of birth, Social Security number or Taxpayer Identification Number, proof of address, or telephone number, and some banks also require an initial deposit. If you are not yet 18, you will also need an identification detail for the other applicant and a signed legal document with the bank from your parent or guardian.

Choose a checking account if you wish to pay bills, write checks, and make debit card transactions with no monthly fees, low or no overdraft fees, and simple free ATM access. However, suppose you're creating an emergency fund or putting money aside for specific goals. In that case, a savings account with a high-interest rate (preferably 0.50 percent or higher) and no monthly fees is the way to go.

You'll likely find lower costs and higher interest rates if you consider online-only banks. Fees and rates are often higher at brick-and-mortar institutions, but they also come with a greater range of services and, of course, in-person assistance.

What to do with your bank accounts

An emergency fund is a financial safety net for unexpected catastrophes and/or unforeseen bills. It should normally include three to six months' worth of expenses, but the 2022 economic crisis and lockdown have prompted many experts to propose up to one year's worth.

It may be tempting to utilize your emergency fund for unrelated or frivolous expenses, so be sure you don't use it for anything other than an actual emergency like losing your job, insurance, car maintenance, or suffering a terrible illness.

While keeping cash in a savings account is the safest option, there are other relatively safe methods to keep a portion of your emergency fund that earns more interest. High-interest savings accounts, money market accounts, and no-penalty certificates of deposit are examples of these.

It's never too early to begin putting money down for your retirement. Start saving for retirement so that you can have a secure future. The longer the money is invested and earns interest, the more value it will have in the future.

Because the money will grow tax-free until you withdraw it in retirement, 401(s) and 403(b) retirement accounts are excellent investments. You can also save it in a tax-deferred retirement plan like an IRA. IRAs are comparable to 401(k)s in terms of tax benefits, but there are some differences in eligibility.

Many teenagers work part-time to begin managing their financial destiny. As a result, employers will send paychecks that can be cashed or placed into a teenager's account via direct deposit. Setting up a direct deposit is a terrific way to get a "taste" of having a bank account. Checking accounts may include a debit card. Debit cards allow multiple deposits and withdrawals, a convenient way to make purchases.

Managing your bank accounts

It is simplest to construct an excellent financial future on a solid foundation. Use these common-sense money management ideas to help you succeed financially.

1) Open a savings account as soon as possible. You'll have a safe location to put your newfound money while also earning interest. But first, know how much money you'd like to put into your savings account. Examine the minimum deposit quantity at your preferred bank and proceed from there.
2) Open a checking account to have a debit card. A debit card is similar to a credit card but with training wheels. Open a checking account to begin using a card and managing your accounts online. You'll be much more prepared when you receive a credit card once you turn 18 if you've spent money with a card rather than cash.
3) Make a basic budget. When creating a modest, realistic budget, start by totaling money sources such as allowances or part-time job pay. Then subtract your monthly costs, including savings account contributions and miscellaneous spending money. As an adolescent,

you will most likely have low monthly expenses. This is a fantastic opportunity to make a budget.

4) Sort out wants from needs. Make a list of what you want and need. It's an essential part of money management, but teenagers frequently disregard it. When your paycheck starts to dwindle, you'll be more likely to conclude that some "needs" are "wants."

How do you deposit cash?

If you have a physical bank or credit union account, you can bring cash to a branch and make a deposit in person. You can deposit cash at any branch of a credit union member of the shared branching network. Banks and credit unions have until the next business day to make your cash deposit available for withdrawal or cover your checks and debits.

ATM deposits are easy, but the cash may not be available in your account immediately after they are made. Most policies (and federal law) enable banks to retain funds for an additional day, with the possibility of a longer stay. Some ATMs will read and count your banknotes as you insert them, while others will ask you to place your cash in an envelope.

There are Online-Only Banks:

1) ACH transfer

The simplest method is to put cash in a bank account and transfer it to your online bank account. There may be a cost associated with sending a wire.

2) ATM deposits

There are online banks that accept ATM deposits. Verify with your bank to check if a particular ATM network is available.

3) Prepaid cards

If your bank does not accept cash at ATMs, look for a prepaid card that you can "cash load" or deposit money on. Another method is to utilize reloadable reload cards with a debit card.

4) Money orders

If your bank offers mail-in deposits, you can buy a money order with cash and mail it.

5) Mobile deposit

This saves time on the mail, but you'll still have to get the money order in person, and some banks don't accept money orders as deposits.

Please note that you can also deposit your money on someone else's account. You can use PayPal, Venmo, Zelle, and Cash Apps.

If you want a non-digital method, checks are still your best bet. Checkbooks can be helpful when you don't want extra fees. Some businesses charge convenience or processing fees for credit and debit card payments. It can also be useful if you want a paper trail because it is traceable, making it easy to locate the record of spending.

How to write a check:

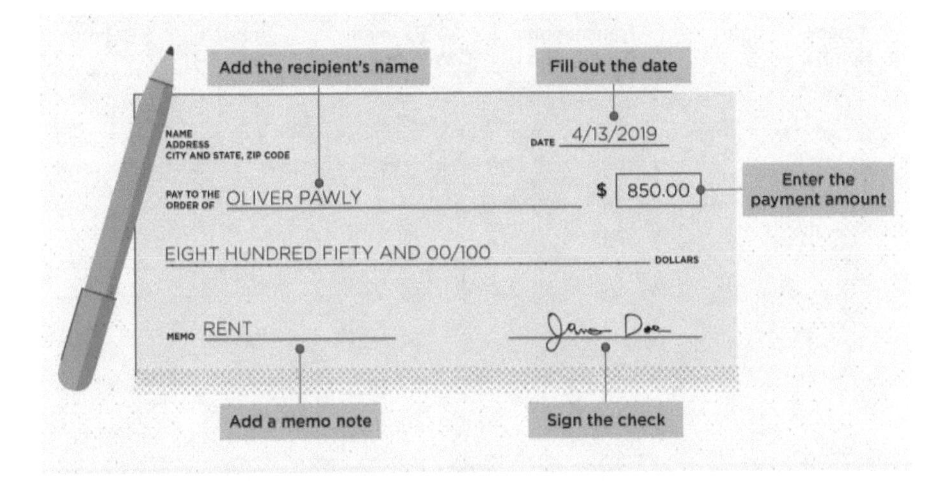

1) Write the date.
2) Write the name of the person or company you want to pay. If you don't know the actual name, you can just put "cash."
3) Write the payment amount in numbers.
4) Then write the payment amount in words.
5) Write your reason or note for the check in the memo.
6) Sign the check.

Checking Your Balance

Checking your balance is a good way to ensure your transaction history matches your bank statement. You'll be able to see any abnormalities, report any potential fraud, and obtain a better grasp of your financial status. If you use checks frequently, you should begin balancing your checkbook.

Large Print Check Register

Check Number	Date	Transaction Description	Payment Withdrawal (-)		Deposit Credit (+)		$ Balance

Please do the following:

1) Make a note of the check number when paying. This also makes it easier to keep track of your checks and reminds you when they need to be reordered.
2) Make a note of the date for future reference. Describe where the payment was made or for what in the "Transaction" field.
3) Subtract any checks, withdrawals, payments, and bank fees from the total amount in your account from the prior transaction, or add in deposits.
4) While it's great to splurge on something you truly want right now, make sure you save money before buying anything. Savings automation isn't new advice, but it works because it eliminates present bias.

5) If you utilize direct deposit, you can separate your paycheck between a checking and a savings account. Another method is to set up automatic deposits from your checking account. This way, you'll be saving a set amount of money regularly without even allowing yourself to spend it on something else.

Recently, a slew of new apps and savings tools have hit the market, promising people new ways to save money. Some of these apps "round up" the amounts from daily expenditures. For instance, if you spend $5.25 at a coffee bar, the app will deposit 75 cents into your savings account.

Next Steps

I may have given you some details about opening a bank account. But let me tell you that there is still other important information you need to know.

I recommend that you do further research. Look into local banks as well as online-only banks. Do your best to compare what each has to offer so you can narrow it down and make the right decision on which one you can start with.

Don't hesitate to give them a call or visit them directly. Make sure, though, that your parents or guardian accompanies you.

Don't forget to read the fine print. That's for your benefit.

Once you have the information you want and the needed requirements, you can go ahead and open your first bank account.

As this chapter has shown, one of the most important things you can do is save money. Do something for yourself and your future while you are still young, and your bank account will provide you with a safe place to keep your money.

However, saving isn't the only thing you can do with your money. One of the reasons you earn money is most likely to spend it in the first place.

How do you know if you're on the right track? How do you make sure you're spending your money wisely?

Chapter Five

Spending Your First Dollar

"Spending money is much more difficult than making money" - Jack Ma.

Whether you have financial responsibilities or not, you have your own expenses as a teen. It's easier to control your spending if you're only relying on your parents for money, but once you start making your own, it can be harder to control.

Spending money is a complex subject. On the one hand, it's fun because you get to buy what you want. However, the other side tells you that you need to be careful when spending.

Two of the major factors on why people fear spending money is they feel they might overspend, and they do not have enough.

They don't have to; you don't have to. This chapter covers how to manage your expenses and spend more conscientiously.

What do you spend money on?

According to recent research, teens spend an average of $174 weekly on discretionary products. So, what are they spending their money on?

Let's face it; most teens love to buy stuff. I don't deny it; I was guilty of some crazy spending habits when I was younger.

And with the advent of online shopping, it seems that the younger generation may be falling prey to impulsive buying or to coin a new phrase, obsessive buying. Before we go any further into this buying trend, why don't you take a look at these other data about teen spending habits:

Teens spend 14 times as much on food as middle-class adults do on food, 8 times as much on books and clothes as middle-class adults do on books and clothes, and twice as much on the entertainment super-category (which includes video games and other electronics, plus movie and concert tickets).

Teens have spent more money on video games in 2019 than at any other time in history. Male teenagers, on average, spend 14 percent of their disposable income on video games, whether purchased or earned in other ways.

17 percent of teenagers between the ages of 12 and 17 claimed to understand how to handle their money, and 24% of teenagers who responded said that they did not know the difference between credit and debit cards.

Why am I showing you these stats? Some of the spending issues may need your closer attention. As we go through the different areas of spending, you can go back to these numbers and check how relevant they are.

Now moving on with the topic, here is a list of stuff teens usually spend their money on. Hopefully with this list, you can identify those that you spend on, and you can evaluate your spending habits.

- Cell phone unit
- Cell phone plan
- Earphones/Headphones
- School supplies
- Car Insurance
- In-app purchases
- Gas
- Snacks
- Toiletries
- Subscriptions
- Video games
- Clothes
- Shoes
- Concert/Event Tickets
- Parties
- Gym membership
- Starbucks
- Mall money
- Car repairs
- Salon services

- Computer/Laptop
- Accessories
- Pet Care
- Art Supplies

What do you think of this list? Does it mirror yours? Or is your list longer?

Now think about how you fund these expenses. Are you paying out of your allowance money? Are you blowing off your earnings? Do you use cash gifts?

Though food has consistently dominated adolescent spending habits for nearly a decade, clothing has now surpassed food as the most important purchase priority for teens. In the fall of 2021, teenagers spent 22 percent of their money on clothing, regardless of income.

The popularity of athletic brands such as Nike, Adidas, and Lululemon exemplifies the trend toward casual clothing, which may have been influenced by the remote school environment throughout the pandemic. However, a recent study shows that only 10% of teenagers prefer to shop at major chains, while 30% prefer to shop at specialty stores.

Food spending is still important for teenagers, and Chick-fil-A has surpassed Starbucks as the top restaurant for this age group. Starbucks' decline could be attributed to its increasingly slow lines as a result of the introduction of mobile orders and the resulting service slowdown.

The entertainment, media, and video game industries have grown in popularity. Because of the ongoing effects of the

COVID-19 pandemic, many more teenagers are spending the majority of their time at home. As a result, their spending is more focused on these industries rather than on concerts and travel. Similarly, online shopping has gained popularity over in-person shopping.

With all this in mind, how do you prioritize your expenses?

Prioritizing your expenses

Managing your spending will take a lot of patience from you. The topmost thing you should consider is knowing the difference between needs and wants.

As you get older, you'll realize that the line blurs between your wants and needs. For instance, you need a car to get to and from, but at the same time, having a car is what you have always wanted. You like the feeling of independence.

So, where does this fall? Is a car a want or a need?

If you struggle distinguishing these two aspects, then read on.

First of all, you need to define the two:

- A need is something that is required in order to live and function.
- A want is something that will enhance your quality of life.

A need, according to these criteria, includes food, clothing, shelter, and medical care, whereas a want includes everything else. These terms, however, are more fluid than they appear at first glance, and some items may appear to fit into both categories. Allowing some time to go by before fulfilling your need for the item is a good trick for dividing wants and needs. Your desire for a necessity grows stronger over time, whereas the desire for a want weakens over time.

Now use the list of expenses I listed earlier (or the one you created). What you can do after is determine to which category each expense belongs to. You can rank the list with categories like "important" or "urgent."

Consider trade-off budgeting. This is intended to encourage individuals to think about fixed money, which is the amount of money that must be paid out every month for necessities, and discretionary money, which is the money that is left over. For example, if you have an emergency car repair this month, you may have to forego your weekly Starbucks treat.

Now, if you get stuck on a specific item and don't know where to put it, ask yourself the following questions:

Do I really require this item in order to live and function?

Is it possible to meet this need at a lower cost?

What would my life be like if this item didn't exist? When you've finished your list of needs, you can add any remaining expenses to your list of wants.

Now it's time to evaluate your list, and then, tweak it.

After you've finished this exercise, go over your list of needs to see if anything can be cut. Will you still require these items in a few years, or even a few months? Can any of your requirements be substituted for a less expensive option?

For instance, you may require clothing, but do you require 10 pairs of designer jeans? Or, while you need a new phone, does it have to be the latest iPhone?

Apply the same method with your list of wants. Which of them are there solely to keep up with others or to look good? Which of your desires was more important to you in the past than it is now?

Which of these are status symbols? Reduce your list until you're left with only the desires that truly add value to your life.

Managing how you spend your money becomes simple now that you know how to tell the difference between needs and wants. Assign dollar amounts to your fixed and non-fixed needs, save money, and use the rest to pay for your wants.

You'll probably have an easier time controlling your impulse purchases in the future. Before you buy something, consider whether it is a necessity or a desire. If the item is a want, consider its importance as well as other wants you've recently purchased before proceeding with the purchase.

One of the most difficult aspects of creating a monthly budget is distinguishing between wants and needs. Follow the steps outlined above to learn how to easily differentiate between these two spending categories. By doing that, you can begin to prioritize your expenses.

Unnecessary Spending

Yes, most of us are guilty of this score. I'm sure your parents, like mine, never tire of scolding you.

"You're wasting money!"

Back in your grade-school days, it was easy for your parents to forgive you about money. Now that you are in your teens, things are a little different.

One reason is that the stakes are always higher. Your 17-year-old self is far more likely to waste money than your 7-year-old self. Consider the difference between expensive video games and sweets.

How do you know if you are wasting money?

Here are definite signs you are wasting money:

1) Buying Impulsively

Impulsive buying is one of the simplest ways to go over budget without realizing it. You believe you know what you need, but that fantastic jacket you just saw is grinning ear to ear at you. You buy it, and your budget is depleted. You must now obtain additional funds in order to purchase what you urgently require, such as food or other necessities.

If you want to conserve money, you must first recognize your impulsive buying habits. Spending money on goods that promise immediate pleasure, status, or recognition from others, whether online or offline, will never help.

2) Buying much too cheap items

Now there's a fine line between cheap and "too" cheap items. When you choose a low-cost item, please make sure that it's something that's durable.

I'm specifically referring to buying anything cheap that will cause you to become bankrupt far sooner than you expect. Electronics are a good example; if you buy used, you may find yourself throwing away that piece of technology within months, even weeks. Are there any assurances? No.

3) Going for special deals and offers

You'll come across a number of special deals, discounts, and coupons whether you're shopping online or offline. $1 things that would normally sell for $10, for example, are incredibly appealing. Brands exploit the fear of losing out as a typical effective tactic to elicit emotional buying responses.

You're essentially wasting money when you buy a $1 product that you'll probably never use. If you buy unhealthy things because they're on sale, you're putting your health at risk. Medical bills will cost you far more in the long run than the money you saved when acquiring that goods.

4) Subscription overload

There may be much enjoyment to be had in them, but they can put a strain on your finances. Because subscription services are set up to charge your credit card automatically, they can do more significant financial harm than other purchases. This situation makes it far too easy to maintain them indefinitely – or even forget you're paying for them.

It's fun every time we subscribe for something, and what's not fun is allowing yourself to accumulate all this and never even find a use for them.

Remember to cancel subscriptions as soon as you stop using them!

Questions to ask before purchasing something

We often buy something without thinking if we genuinely need or want it. It's a great idea to be sure you really need something and that it matches your long-term financial goals before buying it.

That's why you should pause and think hard. Here are some helpful questions to ask yourself before purchasing anything:

1) Can I afford it?

You must ensure that the purchase will not put you in debt. You wouldn't want the amount you pay on this item to take away from something you might actually need. For example, you see a cute trendy dress at the mall. Would buying it make you miss paying your upcoming phone bill? Before you buy, make sure that all bases are covered.

2) Do I need this?

There is nothing wrong with purchasing items. But sometimes, we fool ourselves into thinking we're buying something we need when it's just a want. Consider whether you genuinely require another handbag even though you already have 5, some of them unused.

Planning to splurge on the latest iPhone, even if you have the last year's version that still functions, can be wasteful spending. Some people purchase things not because it's a necessity. Instead, they buy them because they are trendy, on sale, or simply caught your eye.

3) How often will I use it?

Be honest about how often you intend to use something. You may use a coffee maker daily, so purchasing one is more sensible than buying a blender that you may only use once or twice.

You may even go one step further. Ask yourself, will I ever use it?

4) Do I even want it?

Most of us assume we want something when we really want to impress our friends and family. Before you buy something, could you give it some serious thought? You won't regret it.

If you are purchasing something mostly because you assume you "should" have it rather than because you want it, you should reconsider. Evaluate your motivations.

5) Can I borrow it from someone?

If the item is something you won't use very often, it can be worth borrowing instead. It makes no sense to buy anything you can borrow.

If you're not sure whether you'll enjoy a book, borrow it from the library first. Before you buy something, please give it some thought. Who knows? You might discover that you don't need it after all.

6) Is this impulse buying?

Even if we answer yes to all of the above questions, we may still make an impulse purchase. You will suddenly feel that you could have stopped yourself.

Realizing that what you did was due to impulse, the after-shopping high fades, you begin to feel guilty about how much you spent.

You are most likely making an impulse purchase if you go into the store without a list of what you need. Then, you find something at random and buy it.

How should you spend your money?

As early as now, it would be best if you plan on how to spend your hard-earned money. It's highly recommended that you focus first on financial responsibilities. Your parents most likely gave you a financial responsibility or something they want you to pay or contribute to. These "responsibility expenses" might be:

- Car insurance
- Gas for your car
- Plan for your smartphone
- Money when going out with friends
- Driver's license and driver's ED
- Helping out with some household bills, such as electric bills.

But not all your money should be spent on paying bills. It would help if you also had a mixture of things that make you happy and things that will contribute to your future.

Please remember that you will not be a teen forever. Try spending your now spendable cash to make your late teens or early 20s a little simple; your future self will appreciate it.

For example, if you save for and complete a driver's ed course, you'll be eligible for discounted auto insurance for years to come. When you are on your own and paying rent, that will make a difference. There are also other things you could invest in now to benefit you in the near future.

- Laptop/ computer to take for college and to use for job searching
- Used car
- A piece of furniture that you can take to your dorm or first apartment
- Resume building activities

Consider how much money you can save up for things that could make a difference in your life in your 20s as opposed to just spending all of your money on the things you will not use in the future.

I know it can be pretty daunting, but you need to spend your money wisely. This age-old advice from our elders hits the mark.

Making money as a teen is a fantastic experience. It's a liberating sensation, but power comes with many responsibilities. These suggestions will assist you in making sensible financial decisions so that you do not begin your adult life broke.

Here are some tips:

1) Create a spending plan and list all your income and expenses to control your cash flow properly. There are many apps that can help you manage your money.
2) If you eat out for lunch or buy snacks daily, the costs can quickly add up. Making food at home using ingredients you already have can help you save a lot of money. It's fine to dine with your friends once in a while, but doing so frequently can be expensive and not worth the money.
3) Don't spend money on something if you don't have to. Money will entice you to spend it on items that will not genuinely benefit you in the long term. Making the most of what you've got will change your perspective on what's truly important.
4) Go shopping with your parents. This concept will surely make you sigh, but it will demonstrate how complicated spending can be. You might discover that purchasing something in bulk rather than in smaller quantities saves you money. You can also discuss how to obtain and use coupons and discount cards with your parents.
5) Read the fine print before purchasing anything of significant value. There are likely a million reviews and articles on any product or experience you're thinking about purchasing. Do your research; there might be a better choice or a better deal available to save you money.

6) Keep as many receipts as possible if something you purchased is damaged. Receipts are also essential to have on hand if a company gives a reimbursement. The last thing you want is for the item you bought to suddenly stop working and be unable to replace it because you don't have a receipt.
7) When shopping alone, make a list and stick to it. Don't let your second-guessing influence you. Window shopping increases your desire to purchase when you receive your next paycheck or allowance.
8) Don't go for trends. You've seen the current trend and want to join in, right? Never let others influence your financial decisions, and never let others tell you what to do with your money.
9) You don't need to buy everything new, and you don't need to buy a brand new one in terms of clothing, shoes, and electronics. There are shops like eBay that sell gently used products, and you can also go to your local thrift shops to buy second-hand items which are inexpensive and sustainable.
10) You don't have to spend a lot of money on high-end items. Instead, buy top-rated drugstore brands for a fraction of the cost. You should value positive feedback and results over brand recognition.

Using Your Debit Card Wisely

There are three ways in which you can make purchases. You can pay through cash, a credit card, and a debit card.

A person who purchases products or services through cash makes a monetary payment to the provider in the form of bills or coins. Individuals who do not have a bank account or who are attempting to avoid reporting an income tax liability prefer cash payments.

You can use a credit card to make purchases and pay for them later. It's similar to a short-term loan in that regard. More on this topic in Chapter 6.

Now let's talk about debit cards. When you use a debit card, money is deducted immediately from your checking account. These are typically known as "bank cards" or "check cards," and can be used to purchase products or services, as well as to obtain cash from an automated teller machine or a merchant who will allow you to add an additional amount to purchase.

Some people prefer using debit cards over other forms of payment. Let's look at some of the advantages:

1) Obviously, debit cards are useful for shopping and paying bills.

You can use the debit card to make in-person payments, top up a wireless phone, and pretty much any other payment transactions as soon as the funds are available. In most circumstances, sending money to a debit card is faster and easier.

2) A debit card allows you the convenience of not having to carry around cash.

Carrying cash makes you vulnerable to thieves. One of the disadvantages of using cash, especially if you're fully committed to the cash envelope system, is that you'll always be carrying cash—and often a lot of it, especially after payday. At some point, someone will see you pulling out a fat envelope full of crisp 20 dollar bills, and if that someone happens to be a thief, then you know what's coming.

Also, there's a possibility of losing hard money. With a debit card, you can ideally cancel it before it is used. If you lose cash, you're completely out of luck—no way to get it back.

3) You are not likely to go into debt with a debit card.

Compared with a credit card, debit cards are unlikely to give you debt issues. Debit cards are not financial contracts because they are simply a means of accessing one's bank account when used to make a payment. The debit user owes no money to anyone except for any transaction expenses; the purchase was made with their accessible funds.

4) Using a debit card allows you to manage your money more efficiently.

Each month, only put a set amount on your debit card that you may spend for your expenses. This will assist you in limiting your expenditures and sticking to your budget. Overdraft fees will apply if you go above the limit on your debit card, so you'll learn to keep track of your spending.

Debit cards are a great mode of payment. Just remember to keep an eye on pending transactions, protect your card info and be wary of phishing scams.

Next Steps

The next time you go shopping (online or in-person) before you buy that item, step back and ask yourself the questions listed in this chapter. You'll be surprised at how much less you'll be spending.

Spending your first dollar is a crucial money management event in your life and this chapter shows you how important it is to handle your expenses. You did a lot of hard work earning that money; therefore, you should put extra care into how you spend it.

It can be hard to resist temptation. You want to splurge. But that route is never the answer, especially if you want to have a financially secure future.

I hope the details and tips provided give you the foundation for making the right financial decisions. As teens, you may not be known as wise spenders. It's time to remove that notion from people's minds.

The spending habits you build today will carry with you into adulthood. It's hard to break out of habits so starting good ones early will help you start your adult life right.

One of the biggest and most unavoidable things you'll be spending money on as you become an adult is bills.

CHAPTER SIX

PAYING YOUR FIRST BILL

While clothes, shoes, gadgets, and dining out can be easily reduced or eliminated in your budget, bills are financial obligations. They need to be paid; if not, you risk enormous consequences.

You'll take your spending habits into adulthood if you start now. It's difficult to break bad habits, so getting into healthy ones early will help you start your adult life on the right foot. Bills are one of the most important and inescapable expenses you'll encounter as an adult.

You might ask, why do you need to know all this stuff? For the most part, your parents handle this task for the family. But at some point in your teenage life, you won't have a choice but to fulfill this duty.

For example, you must pay your way when you go to college. You risk going into debt and not being able to pay your bills if you don't learn this ability.

Bills that need to be paid

So, let's get the ball rolling by learning about the different kinds of bills you'll need to pay someday. Bills are the due payments that you need to settle for the consumption of some things. Some of the most common bills are the following:

1) Rent or mortgage

Those who don't own a home, called renters, must pay a particular monthly rent. On the other hand, homeowners must pay down the mortgage used to acquire the home.

2) Electricity

It's a bill issued by a local utility to a customer for the electricity used in their home. This bill does not have a fixed amount; the rate is dependent on your monthly consumption.

3) Gas

Gas distribution or transmission companies provide natural gas for their homes, and the charges for those provisions make up a gas bill.

4) Credit card bills

A credit card billing statement is a regular statement sent to you that contains all of your credit card payments, purchases, and other debits and credits for the billing cycle. Your billing statement is sent once a month by your credit card issuer.

5) Water and sewer bill

Your water/sewer bill usually includes four to six charges. Those charges include the fixed water charge, the actual consumption, the fixed charge for sewer, the actual consumption, the service charge, and the water deposit for new customers.

6) Internet service bill

People pay a monthly fee to have internet service delivered to their residence. The wifi-router allows transmission of a wired connection to your devices, such as a phone, TV, laptop, and others, wirelessly.

7) Phone bill

This charge can be for your landline or mobile phone. It's payment for the monthly usage, which is based on your chosen plan.

8) Cable bill

This is for cable usage. Typically, there's a fixed amount too.

9) Subscription services

This includes your subscription to services like the gym, streaming sites, etc. There's a fixed amount according to the plan subscribed to.

10) Insurance

Paying insurance bills can entail paying for medical expenses that insurance does not cover or paying a monthly payment to maintain health insurance coverage.

11) Loans

Many loans are repaid over time with a series of installment payments. These payments typically include interest calculated on the loan's unpaid sum as well as a part of the loan's unpaid balance. Payment of principle is the payment of a portion of the loan's unpaid sum.

Now that you know some of the most common bills that need to be paid, you must also understand how important it is to pay them on time. Paying your payments on time is a vital part of regaining financial control. Knowing when your payments are due and making it a habit to pay them on time can relieve stress, save money, improve your credit score, and allow you to obtain lower-interest credit in the future.

Paying your bill on time

One of the worst traits bill payers have is always procrastinating, which leads to many consequences. As early as now, it would be best if you formed the habit of paying your bills on time to avoid those setbacks.

Here are some of those consequences:

1) You will be asked to pay late payment fees.

Some suppliers may charge this fee when you pay your monthly statement late. As everyone knows, this occurs with missed credit card payments.

Most credit card agreements have specific fees that will be levied. The sum charged will usually be between $15 and $35, depending on the size of your balance. This can be a significant percentage of your balance for modest monthly balances under a few hundred dollars. A single late payment fee is the equivalent of a year's worth of interest on that sum.

A few credit cards, such as the Citi Simplicity® Card, don't impose late fees. The penalty fee is the smallest of the three potential penalties for paying late, and it's merely a one-time fee.

2) You may incur higher interest rates.

This applies to credit cards again. Credit card firms are generally barred from raising your credit card interest rate without giving you 45 days' notice, and they can only do it after the first year.

One significant exception is if you are more than 60 days late on a credit card payment. In this instance, many cards will change your card's APR from the rate you agreed on to the penalty or default rate. The penalty APR will be much higher than the standard interest rate on your card, with most businesses setting this rate between 27 and 30 percent.

The issue with having a penalty rate applied to your card is that most card agreements state that this rate can be charged indefinitely in the future. This has long-term implications for how much holding a balance on your card will cost you in the future. Because not all credit cards charge a penalty rate, it's a good idea to read the fine print of your credit card agreement to see if this is the case.

3) There will be a negative impact on your credit score.

While the late charge is a one-time payment, and the penalty APR usually applies only to that card, late payments of more than 30 days are reported to the credit agencies and appear on your credit record.

The credit score will be impacted by late payments on your credit history. The extent of the reduction will be determined by a number of factors, including how frequently you've missed payments and your previous credit score.

A low credit score lowers your chances of being approved for a credit card, mortgage, or loan in the future. A low score can also impact the interest rate you will pay if you are authorized for a loan with a lower credit score and higher interest rates.

4) You run the risk of getting cut off.

It's critical to take action if you're experiencing difficulties paying your utility bills, such as gas and electricity. Utility companies can cut off your supply.

Contacting your vendors is the best option. Most of these vendors adhere to a code of conduct that states that if you agree to a payment plan with them and stick to it, they will not cut off your supply.

5) Your plan and contract may be compromised.

The account can go into arrears if you do not pay your mobile phone contract. Your mobile provider may disconnect your phone services, which will prevent you from making or taking calls.

The account will default, and the contract will be revoked if you resolve the debt. Following the standard debt collection process, the cell carrier can take measures to recover the overdue account.

6) Your account contract may be placed in default status.

This applies to some loans. You can be in default under the loan contract if you do not make your payments on time and in full. The default might happen right after a missed payment or months later, depending on the conditions of your loan and state or federal legislation.

Your account could go into default with a single missed payment, depending on the creditor and loan type. If you miss numerous payments in a row, your account may be overdue. Defaulting on a loan has different implications depending on the lender and the type of loan.

A defaulted debt may be assigned to the collections department of the lender or sold to a third-party agency in various situations. If you default and the creditor obtains a judgment against you, your salary or tax refund may be tarnished.

Certain forms of loans come with their own set of circumstances. You may not be eligible for further federal loan choices such as forbearance and deferment, additional federal student loans, or alternative repayment plans if you have an existing federal student loan in default. You may be able to rebuild your federal student loan, take it out of default, and get back on track with a repayment plan, unlike some other types of debt.

Of course, there are benefits to paying your bills, especially if you pay them on time or even early. Check out some of them here:

1) You can receive discounts

Depending on the chosen service supplier and where you reside, paying bills before they're due can occasionally result in reductions. In New York City, for example, paying your property taxes early results in a tax reduction. If you obtain service from Marietta Power & Water and pay your account within ten days of the invoice date, you will earn a 10% discount.

If you settle the payment for your healthcare company early or within a particular time frame, you may be eligible for a discount. Check with your service provider or a local government body to discover what kinds of discounts you could be eligible for.

2) You can receive a cut from the interest

If you use your credit card to accumulate debt and pay the minimum amount each month, you're essentially paying interest. If you stick to that payment schedule, you'll be paying off your debt for a long time. Interest is calculated by credit card companies using the average daily balance, which means the more extensive your daily balance is, the more interest you'll pay.

Paying down your credit card debt faster will save you money in the long term. The same is true for your auto loan and home payment. The sooner these bills are paid off, the better. And every amount helps, so don't be disheartened if you can only contribute a small amount.

3) You can get a tax break

Making your mortgage payment early in December may qualify you for a tax credit. Unlike rent, which is usually paid at the start of each month, mortgage payments are made at the end. You can deduct mortgage interest in the current year and apply it to your tax break for that year if you pay your January mortgage payment early in December.

The interest payment for December will be included in your January mortgage payment. Make sure your payment is credited as an interest payment for the year to accomplish this. You may wish to call the mortgage company and inform them of your situation. Note that this method is only applicable to paying your January mortgage in December.

4) You can build your credit

Although sending a credit card bill payment early will not get you bonus points, paying bills on time is a reliable method to establish credit. Your credit score will not be harmed if you pay your bills on time each month.

5) You can get some breathing room

If something goes wrong with your payment, paying bills early will provide you some breathing room. It's possible that your check will go missing in the mail or that your online payment will take a few days to post to your account. By paying your bill early, you can avoid the penalties with late payments.

There may be no more significant benefit to paying bills early than knowing that all of your expenses have been paid and you won't have anything to worry about for the next month. You won't have to worry about coming up with money or dealing with late payment penalties. It will also assist you in developing sound financial habits. After you've taken out the money, you'll need to pay your bills for the month, and you may plan how you'll spend the remaining money.

How to pay your bills

Now it's time for you to know about the different ways to pay your bills. Knowing the different payment channels is helpful because knowing that you have different methods prevents you from missing out on them.

Please check this list:

1) Cash

Of course, this is the most common payment option. You can pay providers directly with hard money. It's one of the easiest and most common forms of payment.

2) Credit card

Some service providers do accept credit cards. While convenient, this type of payment may involve additional fees, especially late payment ones if you are unable to pay the credit card bill on time.

3) Direct debit

It's the simplest, safest, and most convenient way to make recurring payments, so it's commonly used for items like council tax and energy bills. A Direct Debit is a request to your bank from you, giving authority to take payments from your account when they're due for specific services.

4) Checks

Checks are still routinely accepted, especially at larger retailers and for purposes such as bill payment. All you need to do is write the supplier a check so that they can cash it in.

5) Mobile payment

Bills can be paid through the phone utilizing a variety of direct accounts and third-party apps. You can make one-time payments as well as set up autopay for privileged accounts to avoid missing payment deadlines, incurring late penalties, and damaging your credit.

To make your payments a breeze, here are some tips:

1) Check your bills regularly to ensure you don't miss a payment. There may be instances when your due date gets changed. Always ensure that you are being billed appropriately. You can do this by analyzing the bill, whether you receive it by mail or electronically.
2) Sign up for automatic payments, especially for recurring bills. Auto-paying bills can help you avoid missing payments that could harm your credit score. Furthermore, lenders and credit card issuers are more likely to offer you better terms, such as reduced interest rates, if you have a higher credit score.
3) Consolidate your bills by getting them from one provider.
4) Schedule time for paying bills every month or week. That way, it's easier for you to remember the task.
5) Organize bills according to the due date. That way, there'll be no confusion.
6) Allow enough time for your payment to arrive.
7) Sign up to receive bill reminders.
8) Pay bills in advance.

Next Steps

If your parents are still paying for everything, you can offer to pay for one of the bills. You may also donate a predetermined amount for one expense. This will be appreciated by your parents and make you feel responsible and independent. Also, setting money aside for your specific obligations each month enhances your money skills.

Not all details in this chapter are tackled in school, but they highlight the value of responsibility and independence for youngsters. Even if you are not yet tasked with dealing with bills payment at home, you will soon. So, it's best that you are armed with all this knowledge.

One of the things I would like to highlight is that the easiest way to pay your bills is to automate them. You don't have to worry about remembering due dates and making payments on time.

Now, there is another important monthly payment you're going to have to make, and that is for insurance.

CHAPTER SEVEN

YOUR FIRST PREMIUM

As much as we would like to keep unwelcome events from occurring, we have no way of knowing if or when something terrible will occur.

Whether it's due to joblessness, sickness, an accident, or other unforeseen circumstances, these events can have a huge financial impact on us.

In times like this, having insurance is a blessing. Insurance plans can help you pay for life's unexpected occurrences.

What is insurance about?

Insurance is a method of risk management. When you acquire insurance, you are purchasing protection against financial losses that may occur unexpectedly. If something horrible happens to you, the insurance company pays you or anybody you select. If you don't have insurance and are involved in an accident, you could be held liable for all charges.

If you don't have insurance and one of the aforementioned unanticipated events occurs, you may be responsible for all associated charges. Having the appropriate insurance in place for the dangers you may face can make a significant impact in your life.

A written contract between the policyholder (the person or company who purchases the policy) and the insurer (the insurance firm) is known as an insurance policy. The policyholder is not always the insured. An individual or organization can purchase an insurance policy that protects another person or entity (making them the policyholder). When a company purchases life insurance for an employee, for example, the individual is the insured and the company is the policyholder.

You might ask why you need insurance. Insurance is one way to protect your life, your health, and your ability to earn an income and keep a roof over your head when things go wrong. You cannot always rely on your parents to shoulder some of these costs.

Types of Insurance

There are various types of insurance covering everything from your home, pets, business, etc. As you're still a dependent, many of these probably won't apply to you yet, but here are some that do.

Health Insurance

This type of insurance is now required for everyone in the United States. People who don't have insurance have to pay penalties that get more expensive each year.

People purchase health insurance in exchange for coverage of all types of medical care. The majority of plans include doctor's visits, emergency department visits, hospital stays, and prescription drugs.

The concept behind insurance is pretty straightforward. Anywhere you ask, medical care is costly. Most people are unable to cover the entire cost out of their own pockets.

However, if a group of people band together and each person pays a set monthly fee (whether or not they require medical treatment at the time), the risk is spread out across the entire group. Because the burden is shared, each person is shielded from exorbitant health-care expenditures.

There are numerous options for purchasing health insurance, each with its own set of fees and benefits. Given your health demands, age, and employment position, you'll need to explore what possibilities are accessible to you.

Check out the following health insurance options for you:

1) Your parents' health plan

In the United States, children under the age of 26 can remain on their parents' health insurance plan. Even if you're married, live elsewhere, and work, this is true.

2) Short-term health plan

To bridge the gap between school and your first job, many insurance firms provide short-term, or "student," insurance policies. These plans are comparable to COBRA, although they are usually simpler and less expensive.

3) COBRA

The Consolidated Omnibus Budget Reconciliation Act of 1985 aims to keep people from losing their health insurance by allowing them to keep their current plan for a limited time. COBRA was created to protect consumers from losing their health insurance coverage unexpectedly.

4) Individual policy

Purchasing healthcare coverage on your own could be more costly than sharing risk with a wider group (such as other students, employees, etc.). You may have to pay extra if you're considered a greater risk, such as if you smoke or engage in other activities that harm your health.

5) Employer-sponsored plans

The majority of Americans obtain their health insurance in this manner. It is also usually the least expensive choice, as companies frequently contribute to the cost of insurance. Some firms provide health insurance on the first day of employment.

Others may require you to labor for a certain amount of time initially (30, 60, or 90 days).

6) State-sponsored program

If you're under the age of 19 and your family's income falls below a specific threshold, you may be eligible for state assistance through SCHIP (State Children's Health Insurance Program). Benefits vary by state, so contact your state's Department of Health and Human Services for more information.

One of the most essential things you should know about health insurance is pre-existing conditions. Having these conditions should not be a reason for providers to deny you coverage. A pre-existing condition is a health problem you had before the start date of your new health coverage. Examples include asthma, diabetes, and cancer.

Auto Insurance

If you drive, whether you have your own car or you sometimes drive your parents', you will need car insurance.

An auto insurance is a protection toward your car investment. Car insurance protects you from financial damages if you are in an accident, or if your vehicle is damaged in some manner.

Some states mandate you to have minimum liability insurance coverage; however, other states additionally require you to have other forms of coverage, such as uninsured motorist coverage. Premiums are the amounts you pay each month, biannually, or annually to keep your auto insurance policy active, whereas deductibles are the amounts you pay when you file a claim.

The following items are covered by auto insurance:

Vehicle damage, whether your own or that of another motorist

Accident-related property damage or bodily injuries

Medical expenditures and/or burial costs incurred as a result of an accident

What's covered depends on your state's minimum coverage standards as well as any other coverage options you want to include. Except for New Hampshire, every state requires drivers to have a minimum amount of bodily injury and property damage liability coverage.

You will need your parents' help in getting this insurance. They can help you gain coverage in one of two ways:

- by adding you to the family's existing vehicle insurance policy
- by assisting you in purchasing your own policy

Adding an adolescent driver to an existing vehicle insurance policy is likely to be the simplest and least expensive choice of the two. Your parents will still need to cosign for you to get your own coverage. They'll likely pay higher premiums due to your higher risk status as a novice driver. But this still depends on your state's insurance requirements.

Now before you go ahead and ask your parents for help, here are some tips for saving on car insurance:

1) If you get good marks at school, you can inquire about student discounts.
2) You can examine the possibility of receiving a discount for completing a driver's education or defensive driving course.
3) Your parents can consolidate their auto and house insurance plans with the same company.
4) If affordable, they can increase their deductibles on your insurance policy.
5) If you qualify for discounts, you may enroll in automated bill payment and electronic document delivery.

Life Insurance

As a teen, life insurance may seem impractical at this point in your life. However, it's something that you should consider.

A contract between you and an insurance provider is known as life insurance. In exchange for your premium payments, the insurance company will pay your beneficiaries a lump sum known as a benefit after you die. Your recipients are free to spend the funds for whatever they like.

Guaranteed insurability, which is an option on permanent life insurance plans, is one of the most prevalent reasons for youngsters to buy life insurance. It permits a person who is already covered to buy more coverage without having to certify their health status again. The specific life insurance policy specifies the amount of coverage that can be added and at what intervals.

Expenses for medical and funeral services is another reason to get life insurance. Unexpected losses, regardless of age, can be financially draining. Funerals typically cost between $8,000 and $10,000. That doesn't include any medical expenses incurred.

You might ask what happens if you get life insurance while you are still young and healthy? The premium will be cheap to begin with and will remain low during your coverage.

Additionally, when you get older, you can add more coverage to your plan without having to update your health status. As a result, if you have a health problem, getting life insurance will not be an issue. You will be able to keep your present coverage and add to it.

Now, let's look at examples of life insurance you can get.

1) Child Rider

A child rider is an addition to your parents' existing life insurance policy. You and your parents will have to make a decision once you reach a certain age. You have the option of converting the child rider into a permanent life insurance policy or terminating the coverage. A child rider is a smart place to start if you're unsure about life insurance at this stage in your life.

2) Term Policy

A term policy is a standalone life insurance policy. Term life insurance policies protect you for a set period of time (usually 5 to 30 years). After that period has passed, the policies can be renewed, but your health may be evaluated, and your premiums may increase.

3) Permanent Policy

Consider a permanent life insurance policy if your primary goal in purchasing life insurance is to ensure insurability. Permanent life insurance is intended to stay with a person indefinitely. There are no temporal limits on when the plan must be renewed or re-evaluated.

Long-term disability insurance

This is one sort of insurance that most of us believe we will never need. And this is especially true for someone as young as you. However, we cannot avoid life's curveballs.

Figures from the Social Security Administration show that one out of every four individuals entering the workforce will become disabled and unable to work before reaching retirement age. So, it's worth checking out whether this type of insurance can apply to you or not.

Long-term disability insurance protects your income in the event you are unable to work due to illness or injury. While short-term disability insurance normally only lasts two years, long-term disability insurance can last five to ten years, if not all the way until retirement.

Cancer, neurological or musculoskeletal diseases, and asthma are just a few examples of long-term disability. They could also include injuries sustained as a result of a fall or an automobile accident.

Long-term disability insurance comes in two varieties:

1. Any-occupation disability insurance offers benefits only if you are unable to work any employment for which you are reasonably qualified due to illness or accident. This is more difficult to prove, and receiving payment is more difficult, but it is often less expensive than own-occupation disability insurance.
2. Own-occupation disability insurance defines a disability as an incapacity to work in your usual occupation and pays out even if you are able to work another job.

Now let's go into the advantages of purchasing this insurance for teens like you.

First, if you get a private policy, it means your premiums will be locked in at a reduced rate, which is fantastic when you get into your 30s, 40s, and beyond. If you try to get an LTD policy in your 40s, you may find yourself with a monthly premium the size of a vehicle payment.

Second, if something serious sidelines you for six months in your mid-30s, an LTD policy you currently own will come in handy. However, if you wait until later to get a policy, you will not only have missed out on the opportunity to take benefit of it, but it will also likely not cover any future health conditions that are comparable to those you had before purchasing the insurance.

Third, the same goes when you are much older. If you've reached a particular age, no matter how much you're ready to spend, you won't be able to get coverage since the insurer will deem your situation too hazardous to insure.

Insurance Reminders

Some reminders for getting life insurance:

1) You should only get the insurance that you need for the amount you want to cover.
2) You may want to go for lower premiums but higher deductibles if you can afford it.

Take note:

lower deductibles = higher premiums

higher deductibles = lower premiums

3) Take the time to canvas and compare insurance options before you select one. Seek advice from your parents and other older adults.
4) Because costs vary, you should obtain quotations from multiple providers before deciding which one to apply to for coverage. You might also engage with an independent insurance agent that represents a number of different insurance companies and can assist you in finding the greatest coverage at the best price.
5) Consider the following:
   - Monthly premium you will pay

- Your co-pay, deductibles
- What is covered
- Type of plan and provider network

6) Lock in Temporary Coverage

If the underwriting procedure for the policy you're buying will take a few weeks or longer, you can usually secure interim coverage by including a check with your first premium payment with your application. While you wait for your application to be approved, you will have coverage and peace of mind. Inquire with your life insurance agent about this possibility.

Next Steps

You can ask your parents about their insurance plans and see if you're included in them. If you prefer this route, you may ask them to add you in their health insurance plan. Apart from what you need right now, like health insurance, think and plan ahead for other types of insurance, ones you may need in the future. This would be a great addition to your financial goals.

Please remember that it's better to be prepared for something bad and have nothing happen than not having anything ready when it happens.

That's what this chapter is about. This section tells you that even at your age, it's best to always come prepared.

Insurance may seem like a useless expense when things are going well, but you'll be grateful you have it when things go wrong. And the reality is that you never know when things will go wrong. So, insurance is always handy to include in your financial plans.

And now that you all have this information about insurance and other money matters, it's also time to think about how to protect yourself and your finances.

Chapter Eight

Getting Your First Credit Card

You sometimes wonder why your next-door neighbor who isn't rich drives a great-looking car. Not a lot of people have tens of thousands of dollars to pay for a car outright, but they can afford to pay a few hundred a month. This is how debt can help you achieve your financial goals more quickly, even if you don't have the funds. However, if you're not careful, you can find yourself without a car and owing more than the vehicle is worth.

You may be told that having debt is wrong. That's not true. It's how you handle debt that may become your undoing.

Having credit and debt isn't wrong. They can actually help you.

What are credit and debt?

Credit is defined as the capacity to borrow money with the promise of repaying it later, usually with interest. You could require credit to buy something or use a service that you can't afford right now.

Credit cards, as well as home, vehicle, and school loans, are the most frequent types of credit. You must apply for credit, and lending institutions (such as banks or mortgage firms) assess the amount you are permitted to use based on your personal financial history.

On the other hand, debt occurs when a person or one party borrows something from another, usually money. Many businesses and individuals utilize debt to finance significant expenditures that they otherwise would not be able to make. A debt agreement gives the borrowing party a chance to borrow money on the agreement that it be repaid at a later date, usually with interest. Debt can also be from unpaid obligations like overdue utility bills, medical bills, unpaid taxes, etc.

So, how do these two connect? Credit is money you borrow from a bank or financial institution. The amount you borrow is your debt.

Before a bank or financial institution will lend you money or grant you credit, they will usually need to check your credit score/ credit report.

Importance of Good Credit

Your credit history can impact your ability to obtain loans and credit cards. It can also influence choices made by insurance providers, landlords, utilities, and employers.

Many organizations analyze your credit history to anticipate your future financial actions because it shows how you've handled debt in the past. As a result, when you apply to borrow money, get a credit card, or rent a place, your credit history could be examined. Great credit scores can indicate that you are responsible and follow responsible financial practices, such as paying your payments on time. Low credit ratings, on the other hand, may create the opposite image.

Maintaining good credit makes it easier to sign a lease, buy a home or car, subscribe to a phone plan, and acquire a student loan, among other things. When it comes to setting up utilities, having good credit can save you cash through the form of reduced interest rates, waived fees, and no down payments.

What is a credit score?

Credit can refer to borrowing money or receiving anything valuable, such as a car, with the promise to repay later often with interest.

Your credit report includes personal details like your work and previous and present addresses, as well as a history of your financial conduct. The report shows how many open accounts you have, current balances, payment history, including late and missing payments, loans you've taken out and their outstanding sums, and any financial disturbances such as bankruptcy or foreclosure.

Your credit score is normally a three-digit value anywhere from 300 to 850. It condenses your credit history and other aspects of your credit report into a shortened form that financial companies can use to assess your creditworthiness.

Building credit

Most people start out with a disadvantage in terms of building credit. It takes credit to develop credit, and without a significant credit history, it might be tough to qualify for the credit cards or loans you need to get started. Fortunately, you may start establishing credit while you're still in high school.

1) Get a job.

Well, getting a job doesn't immediately help you build credit, but money is an important component in obtaining credit, and your employment experience, like your credit history, tends to improve over time. Earned money is a big part of getting credit, and as you obtain more experience, your job history will increase.

2) Become an authorized user.

If you're under the age of 18, you can have an adult add you as an authorized user on one of their credit cards. You are permitted to keep and utilize the adult's credit card; however, you will not be the principal cardholder. The responsible card use of the principal card user can help you improve your credit.

3) Get a secured credit card.

If you're already 18, another option for establishing a credit history from scratch is getting a secured credit card. Secured credit cards need a security deposit that would dictate your line of credit. A security deposit of $200 would get you a $200 credit limit. Although your card is tied to cold cash, you still use it when you make a purchase and make monthly payments just like a normal credit card does.

4) Apply for a student credit card. If you're about to enter college, a student credit card is a terrific place to start. Student credit cards offer fewer qualification restrictions and no annual fees. Student chrome gives cash back for good grades, 2% cashback on up to $1,000 in expenditures per quarter at gas stations and restaurants, and a cashback matching the first year.
5) Use credit cards wisely.

When you do get a credit card, you'll need to use it responsibly for a long time to maintain and improve good credit. This involves paying your bills, keeping your balance low, and paying off your entire balance. Monitoring your credit reports and scores for inaccuracies and indicators of fraud as you improve your credit is a smart practice, as it will help you keep your hard-earned creditworthiness.

6) Pay bills on time.

Late payments can be recorded on your credit report for up to 7 ½ years. Pay up your bills as soon as possible and prevent missed payments.

7) Strategically pay off credit card balances.

Your credit usage is the percentage of your credit limits that you are currently using. Use no more than 30% of your credit limit on any card, and the lesser the better. Less than 7% is used by the highest achievers.

When the card issuer submits your balance to the credit bureaus, make sure it's low, because that's what's used to calculate your score. To keep your debt low, pay down the balance before the payment cycle finishes or pay numerous times throughout the month.

Be careful with debt

Debt comes in a variety of sizes and shapes. We remove the pain of paying when we utilize credit cards. That is, we do not have to feel as if we are wasting money. Sometimes we simply swipe our card through a machine, while other times we use our phones.

All of this is offered as a convenience; however, the real objective is to make spending easier. When spending is so simple, it's all too easy to go overboard and wind up in debt. We lose financial freedom, flexibility, and peace of mind when we are in debt because we owe someone money.

If you have a bad credit history, that might have more ramifications than expected. A poor credit history not only pertains to higher interest rates and lesser loan chances, but it can also make it difficult to find homes and obtain certain services. In some circumstances, it can work against you when looking for work.

Credit cards (or other kinds of debts) can be useful tools provided they are used appropriately, with the necessary self-control, and for a specified purpose. Otherwise, sticking to cash and debit cards while saving for larger purchases will improve your financial health significantly.

Credit cards will almost certainly be your initial debt exposure.

Credit card companies provide credit cards to high school students, and you can even apply for one when you are 18 years old. But a lot of teens still don't understand how to manage their money and drown in debt at an early age. You must understand the benefits and disadvantages of having a credit card as a teen.

Benefits of teens having credit cards:

- It will be an excellent way to expose you to the concept of money management.
- Carrying credit cards can teach teenagers valuable lessons. You will discover about credit scores, bill payments, debt repayment, and much more.
- Credit cards are a useful tool for teens if used appropriately and carefully.
- Having a credit card means you don't need to carry cash or ask for money. It also assists you in times of crisis, such as automotive problems or medical emergencies.
- Credit cards are a wonderful way to establish credit. Building a credit history is beneficial to your future because it can assist you with renting apartments, obtaining vehicle loans, and other things.

Disadvantages of teens having credit cards:

- Some teenagers may be wasteful and negligent with their money. They may seriously harm their credit score in the future. They may overlook monthly payments or exceed their credit limitations.
- Most teenagers are impulsive shoppers. If they have access to a credit card, they may not hesitate about wasting money on something they don't need, resulting in significant debt.
- Many teenagers have shared credit cards with their parents. Parents may end up in more debt than they intend as a result of their teenager's imprudent purchasing.
- When using a credit card, you may not feel as if you are spending "real" money.

Using your credit card responsibly

It's easy to fall into the habit of paying for things with a credit card. Which can be an easy and quick method to pay. But what about the rest of your credit card usage? Is the way you use your credit card helping or hurting your credit?

Follow these general guidelines to keep your finances safe:

1) Read and understand your credit card agreement. Always read the credit card customer agreement and account opening disclosures before opening a new credit card account. You will know what to expect in terms of fees, due dates, interest rates, and other details.

2) You can avoid fees and fines when you pay your credit card minimum payments each month. Paying the bare minimum will only keep your account in good standing, but you will still be charged with interest on that balance. The Consumer Financial Protection Bureau advises people to pay more than the suggested minimum.
3) Make timely payments. Missed or delayed credit card payments can harm your credit, as well as result in late penalties and interest rate increases. To ensure that you pay on time, try to set up automatic payments or electronic reminders. Your payment record has a significant impact on your credit scores.
4) Maintain below your credit limit. Use only the credit that you truly need. Keep your credit limit as low as possible. Your credit usage ratio could have an impact on your credit ratings. According to the Consumer Financial Protection Bureau, you should never use over 30% of your credit card limit.
5) Examine your monthly statements for accuracy. If you regularly check your credit card transactions and statements, whether online or in the mail, will help you stay on top of how you spend your money. It can assist you in identifying transactions that you are unfamiliar with. This could assist you to avoid being a victim of fraud.
6) Keep track of your credit. Maintaining a careful watch on your credit is always a good idea. Monitoring your credit might assist you in staying on track. It's also another tool

for detecting inaccuracies and potential fraud efforts that could harm your credit.

> **There are other forms of credit you might encounter. One is student loans.**

As a high school senior, you've probably begun to consider how you'll pay for college. You may be eligible for scholarships or other assistance based on merit. If not, you'll almost certainly have to borrow money to enroll in a four-year college.

While borrowing student loans may be contentious right now, there are still compelling reasons to do so:

- Federal student loans aren't the worst financial product on the market because they have low fixed interest rates and numerous repayment alternatives.
- Student loan interest is tax-deductible, but most types of debt are not.
- Student loans make higher education possible for millions of students.
- Student debts can lead to improved wages and job satisfaction throughout a person's career.

A lot of people desire to go to college, but financing a post-secondary degree can be challenging. Despite financial aid, paying for school can be difficult. Student loan alternatives can help. There are other actions you can do for funding your education, such as:

1) Apply for more scholarships.

Thousands of scholarships are available to college students, and they are funds that you do not have to repay. Scholarships can be obtained from several places, including educational establishments, foundations for nonprofits, charitable organizations, and companies.

2) Enter Programs for Work-Study.

Federal Work-Study is a program that lets students obtain money on campus to help pay for education. Before you begin, become familiar with the limitations of these applications. You may be restricted in the number of hours you can work and only be authorized to get a certain amount of money. Work-study programs may not be available at some schools.

3) Apply for grants.

Federal grants, like scholarships, are not repaid. Many grants are dependent on financial needs, so you'll need to show that you have financial constraints that make going to school difficult. Because of the need-based component, federal grants are comparable to federal student loans.

4) Get tuition installment plans or payment plans.

Colleges and universities help students to develop payment plans that stretch out a tuition shortfall throughout their academic year. For example, if a student has a $3,000 shortfall, financial aid at their school may allow them to stretch it out over ten months.

5. Go to a community college instead of a big university.

Community colleges save you money since it is generally lower than big colleges and universities.

Apart from student loans, you can consider the following:

1) Car loans

Most of us require a car to fulfill our daily activities. A car loan might assist you in getting on the road. A car loan is a type of personal loan used to buy a car. Lenders lend you the funds needed to purchase a vehicle in exchange for monthly payments on top of the money you pay in interest, usually in monthly installments until the debt is paid off.

2) Personal loans.

Personal loans can be used for anything. You can normally do whatever you want with the money, although some lenders have restrictions. They're harder to obtain than credit cards, and they often have their own set of rules.

3) Mortgage.

It is a loan that is utilized to purchase a house. Mortgages allow you to borrow a significant sum of money and repay it at a low rate of interest. You can only use the money loaned to you with a mortgage to buy, refinance, or repair your home.

Home-equity lines of credit. HELOC functions similarly to a credit card, but it uses your home as collateral. A HELOC can be utilized, repaid, and reused if the account is active, usually for 10 to 20 years.

It would help to know about secured and unsecured loans.

A secured loan is backed by collateral or a guarantee. Mortgages and car loans are types of secured loans. If you don't repay your loan, the bank has the right to take your guarantee as payment. A repossession can last up to seven years on your credit report.

An unsecured loan may not need a guarantee, but you will still be charged with interest and other fees. Unsecured loans may have higher interest rates than secured loans. This sort of borrowing includes student loans, personal loans, and credit cards.

Good vs. Bad Debt

Now, it's good for you to understand the differences between good vs. bad debt. You may have heard your parents, neighbors, and other adults talk about the advantages of taking on "good" debt or the dangers of taking on "bad" debt. Let's look into the differences.

What is good debt?

Low-interest debt is "good" debt since it helps you build wealth or income over time. Student loans are one example of beneficial debt. Student loans are considered good debt because you are investing in your education and working toward a certification or degree that will likely lead to higher lifetime earnings than someone who does not pursue a credential or degree, justifying the need to borrow the money. However, too much debt of any form can rapidly become bad debt.

Good debt examples include:

- Mortgage
- Home Equity
- Small Business Loan
- Student Loan

These good debts allow you to better handle your money, enhance your wealth, acquire what you need, and deal with unforeseen circumstances. Each of the debts above may put you in a financial constraint at first, but eventually, you'll gain in the long term for borrowing the funds.

Now, what do we mean by bad debt?

Any debt that prevents you from achieving financial success is considered "bad." When used improperly, credit cards are frequently regarded as a kind of bad debt (and they may be). Credit cards are classified as bad debt since many credit businesses are predatory, which means:

1) They have hefty interest rates on several of them (around 25-30 percent).
2) Some organizations may push you to pay only the minimum statement balance instead of paying in full every month, which will stretch your debt even further (and rack up a lot of interest)!
3) Some businesses will give "rewards" or "incentives" for using your credit card. This can lead to you spending money you don't have.

Having a credit card isn't a problem if you have a high-interest credit card and pay off your balance each month.

However, if you use a high-interest credit card and merely pay the minimum balance each month instead of paying it off, your debt will quickly accumulate (due to compound interest), making repayment much more difficult and expensive.

With this in mind, you should consider comparing products from different banks and credit card providers. Look for lower fees and interest rates.

Also, read the fine print. Ensure that before you sign up for anything, you know and understand all the nitty gritty details, including your debt-to-income ratio, which will help you know if you have too much debt.

Apart from credit cards, here are other examples of bad credit:

- Payday Loans
- Car loans

Basically, if the item from the loan loses value the moment you own it, it's considered bad debt.

Please note that sometimes, things aren't so black and white when identifying whether a debt is good or bad. You need to make your own judgment based on your financial situation. For instance, a car loan may be a good idea if that's the only way you can get to work to earn money.

Here are some healthy credit habits you can practice:

1) Pay bills on time

Paying your bills on time is the most crucial thing you can do to keep your credit score high. A balance on your credit card is not a good thing. Any payment that is late by more than 30 days will appear on your credit report for seven years.

2) Keep credit utilization low

Your credit card balances are compared to your credit limits to determine credit utilization. The lesser your credit use, the better your credit score. In general, maintaining your credit use below 30% will protect your credit score; individuals with the best credit scores have credit utilization ratios in the low single digits.

3) Check your credit score regularly

Knowing your credit score and how it has changed is always useful since it helps you understand the impact of your actions on your scores. Furthermore, checking your credit score on a regular basis will help you spot any potential difficulties and correct the course if you're straying off track. A growing credit score is excellent news if you're working to improve your credit.

4) Apply for new credit only when needed

A high number of recent credit applications will hurt your credit score. A hard inquiry is a request for your credit report made by a lender every time you apply for a loan or credit. So unless it's truly necessary, don't pursue additional credits.

5) Have an emergency fund to pay for large, unexpected expenses

It's a good idea to place money aside every month for an emergency fund in addition to making monthly contributions to your savings account. If your financial condition changes, you'll be able to fulfill your credit commitments and unforeseen bills.

Next Steps

It's best that you study up on the different ways to build up your credit and read more about loans. Now if you decide to get a credit card, charge a monthly bill, and pay it off in full each month. This develops the habit of paying the bill on time and in full. Of course, charge only what you can pay off.

Yes, getting a credit card is exciting. You feel like a grown-up when you start charging when you go to shops and restaurants. But remember the important lessons this chapter has shared.

Credits and debts require utmost responsibility on your part. Managing your debts and credit well will set you up for a good future.

Another way to be responsible for your money, is to invest wisely. If you choose this route, you will be able to make money on the money you put aside. But be careful, if not managed properly, you could lose all of your hard earned and invested money.

CHAPTER NINE

MAKING YOUR FIRST INVESTMENT

What do typical 16-year-olds do? At this age, most of them are busy entering the social world of friendships and romantic relationships. But not this 16-year-old.

He had a different focus. Sudarshan Sridharan dabbled in stocks.

Sridharan is in charge of his parents' retirement funds, which total roughly $250,000. Although it may appear to be a hazardous retirement strategy, and few people would recommend giving a child so much financial power, Sridharan's parents banked on early success.

Since mid-2013, Sridharan's stock picks had gained more than $43,000. According to financial data supplied by the family, Sridharan's investment in Tesla (TSLA) alone resulted in a $17,000 profit. This profit is on top of the $14,600 gains from Google (GOOGL) stock and $5,600 from Netflix (NFLX). All of these transactions were made using his parents' investing account.

Why am I mentioning Sridharan's success story? I want you to know that age doesn't matter. It's never too early to invest.

You may not have the good fortune that Sridharan began with, but you can have plenty of opportunities for financial growth if you try a hand in investments.

While most people begin investing as adults, starting as a teen can give you a tremendous advantage in terms of saving for the future and learning important financial principles. Investing may appear difficult, but getting started is simpler than you might expect.

Investing as part of your financial plan

Why is investing at a young age a good idea?

Individuals who begin investing as teenagers rather than later in life have a significant advantage over their peers in terms of potential profits and knowledge gained through investment. The sooner you start investing, the longer your money will work for you.

Investing as a teen not only helps young individuals plan for the future financially but also teaches them financial literacy. Personal finances are a cause of stress and concern for many people. According to the Financial Industry Regulatory Authority (FINRA), 53% of Americans consider their finances to be a source of anxiety, with respondents aged 18 to 34 showing the highest levels of stress. By developing financial literacy from a young age, you can feel more confident and less anxious concerning finances later on.

When you invest early and lose money, you'll have more time to recuperate. An investor who begins investing later in life has less time to recuperate his losses. As a result, early investments have more time to rise in value.

You also acquire the habit of saving more when you start investing at a young age. You get more in the future if you invest more. Following that thought process, you will save more money by cutting out unnecessary expenses and investing the money you save.

Investing enhances risk-taking ability. According to studies, young investors are more risk-averse than older investors. Adult investors are often conservative and desire stability; therefore, they shun high-risk investing opportunities. "Bigger the risk, more the gain," as the adage goes. With great risk-taking capacity, the likelihood of generating excellent returns at an early age increases.

An investment made at a young age is beneficial. You will never need to borrow money and become someone's debtor if you have extra money invested. You become a creditor if you have money parked in the correct investment avenues at the right age.

Compounding returns result from early investments. Over time, the time value of money grows. Regular deposits made from a young age can provide significant benefits when it comes time to retire. Your money will increase substantially. Due to early investments, you can buy items that others may not be able to afford at that age. This puts you ahead of others who opt to invest later in life.

Your investment account earnings can be used to help you pay for college, buy a property, have a family, explore the world, open a business, and more. Not only that but when you invest from a young age you increase the likelihood of achieving financial stability earlier. Saving for retirement in your twenties rather than your forties is always a better option. Life after retirement is more difficult than it has ever been, therefore planning for it now will result in a happier life after retirement.

The sooner you begin, the easier it is to accumulate riches. Yes, you will experience some difficulties investing early in life due to a lack of funds. But you can't wait until things are convenient for you.

Investment Basics

There is a lot that goes into investing, and it can be overwhelming, especially if you are young and don't fully get it. But knowing how to invest will give you a head start to reach your financial goals and financial literacy.

It would help for you to know the following:

1) Compound interest

Examine compound interest in much the same approach you would consider the "snowball effect." A snowball starts off small but grows in size as more snow is added. It gets bigger at a faster rate as it increases. Compound interest is the interest generated on the original amount plus interest accumulated. You not only get interest on your initial deposit, but you also earn interest on the interest.

A = P(1 + r/n)^nt

That's the formula for compound interest, which includes the principal sum. Here's the breakdown:

A - the investment/future loan's worth, including interest

P - represents the original investment (the initial deposit or loan amount)

r - annual interest rate (decimal)

n - the number of times that interest is compounded per unit

t - time spent investing or borrowing money

Check out this example:

Let's say you have $5,000 deposited in your bank account with an annual interest rate of 5%. This is compounded monthly.

The value can be calculated in this manner:

P = 5000

r = 5/100 = 0.05 (decimal)

n = 12

t = 10

If we plug these numbers into the above formula, you will have this:

A = 5000 (1 + 0.05 / 12) (12 * 10) = 8235.05

Thus, your investment balance after a decade is $8,235.05.

2) Risk and rewards

There is no such thing as a perfect investment; you must compare the possible reward vs the risk to determine whether it is worthwhile to put your money in jeopardy. Recognizing the link between risk and return is a critical component in developing your investment philosophy.

Investments with lower risks like cash, saving accounts, bank certificate of deposit, bank money market accounts, and savings and protection have low returns while government bonds, stocks, bonds, and mutual funds have high returns but high risks. Collectibles have one of the greatest returns on investment but also the highest risk. Since you are still young, you try to build a strong foundation first before deciding to take high risks. Yes higher rates are tempting, but there is no guarantee that it will be a successful investment.

3) Importance of portfolio diversification

Diversification ensures that you are not placing "all of your eggs in one basket." Diversifying and broadening your stock portfolio is important since it protects your investing assets from becoming overly concentrated in one firm or area.

Mutual funds are an excellent method to diversify your money. You should diversify your investments in terms of both companies and industrial areas. Stocks, bonds, cash, real estate, gold, and other commodities are examples of investments in which you can spread your money.

4) The stock market and how it works

The stock market is an area wherein stocks and bonds are "traded," or bought and sold. The idea is to acquire the stock, hold it for a while, and then sell it for more than you paid for it. Investors who hold stock for 15 years or longer are more likely to prosper in the market. Stocks are your investments in the long-term. But there are no assurances.

Stocks are units of ownership in a firm that raises funds by selling stock. Companies sell stock to raise funds for research into new ways to create things and to grow their products and services. Businesses raise funds in the same way as the federal government does by selling bonds.

How does it work? When you purchase stock, you become a shareholder, which implies you now own a "portion" of the company. If the company's profits increase, you "share" in those increases. If the company's profits decline, so will the value of your stock. You would lose money if you sold your stock on a day when the price of that stock fell below the price you bought for it.

Every day, prices in the stock market rise and decrease. When you invest in the stock market, you hope that the stock will become much more valuable over time than the price you paid for it.

Most individuals realize the importance of investing, but many may not have considered investing for or with their teenagers. Getting you involved in investing at an early age can help you develop wealth and prepare financially for the future, as well as provide you with the financial literacy you will need to succeed later in life.

The most common misperception about investing is that it is only for the old and the wealthy. That could have been true in the past. But that barrier is no longer present, thanks to organizations and services that have made it their mission to make investment opportunities available to everyone, even for teens with limited funds to invest.

In fact, with so many investment opportunities now available to beginners, there's no need to miss out. That's wonderful news because investing is a great method to build money.

What to know before you start investing?

1) Your goals and time horizon. Consider your investment goal as well as your time horizon, or the period of time you will have to invest before achieving those goals. If

your time horizon to your goal is limited, investment may not be the ideal answer for you.

2) Learn the fundamentals of investing. Investing, like any new endeavor, can be intimidating at first. However, once you learn the principles of the stock market and how to invest in stocks, it becomes pretty simple. Read about investing so that you understand how it works, how to prevent common pitfalls, and the best practices to adopt.
3) Discover your investing personality. Discovering your investing personality is another crucial step in the process. Do you like to take chances? Then growth investing could be ideal for you. Do you enjoy being compensated then consider dividend-paying stocks? Do you enjoy a good bargain? You might be a natural value investor.

As you learn more about investing, you'll figure out what interests you the most, which is crucial to staying invested over time and reaping the benefits of compound interest. As you learn more about how to invest the money as a teenager, you'll most likely choose between active and passive investment.

4) Find out which investments are best for you. Start to learn how to research stocks. Choose a couple that intrigue you (both financially and otherwise) and begin researching the company. Examine its financial statements to determine whether the company has the flexibility to weather the expected economic downturns.

5) Create a brokerage account and deposit money into it. It's time to open and fund a brokerage account when you're ready to begin investing. An online brokerage account can be opened by anyone who is at least 18 years old. Those who are younger than that will require the assistance of a parent.

Parents can open a brokerage account or a custodial account on their teen's behalf. The procedure is straightforward and usually takes around 15 minutes. A Roth IRA for kids is a terrific method to start saving if you have earned income.

6) Diversification and risk tolerance. Every investment carries some risk, and the market is unpredictable, fluctuating up and down over the years. It's critical that you grasp your risk tolerance. This entails determining your comfort level with risk and your tolerance for volatility. When it comes to investing, it's best not to put all of your eggs in one basket. Diversify instead. You can lessen investing risk by spreading your money across multiple investments.

What can you invest in?

It can be tough to know where to begin investing when there are so many options available, all of which carry varying amounts of risk. The following are some of the most frequent investments available to teenagers, as well as some of the drawbacks to be aware of.

1. High-Yield Savings Accounts

It is the simplest approach for a teen to begin earning money. Savings accounts have always existed, but more financial institutions are now offering high-yield savings accounts, which pay a higher interest rate than a conventional account. Your money will increase faster with a higher interest rate than in a traditional savings account. In comparison to other assets, even high-yielding savings accounts offer very modest rates of return.

2. Certificates of Deposit

CD is a savings account-like banking product that allows a teen to receive interest on their money. The main distinction is that CDs require you to leave your money in the account for a certain number of months (or even years) in order to collect the stated interest rate.

Then, when the CD matures, you'll receive your money back in addition to the income collected on your account. CDs, like savings accounts, are regarded as a risk-free investment since the money is protected by the Federal Deposit Insurance Corporation (FDIC). However, the disadvantage is that your money is effectively locked up for a period of time.

3. Stocks

Stock is a way to buy a share of a publicly listed company's ownership (also known as "equity"). You become a shareholder and part-owner of a corporation when you buy a stock. Investors can profit from dividends paid by corporations to their shareholders as well as capital gains when the stock's value rises. However, stocks are volatile assets, which means they can see significant price changes in a brief span of time.

4. Bonds

Bond is a financial instrument that is used to secure debt. When you buy a bond, you're effectively lending money to the firm or government that issued it. While bonds may not be as thrilling as stocks to a teen, they are often more reliable assets that contribute to a well-diversified portfolio. Due to the interest payments made by the bond issuer over a predetermined period of time, bonds often provide a fixed income.

5. Mutual fund

It's a form of investment organization that pools money from a number of different participants to produce a well-diversified portfolio. Each investor owns a piece of the fund and participates in its gains and losses. Regardless of when they were placed, all mutual fund transactions are settled at the end of each trading day.

6. ETFs

Exchange-traded funds are another sort of pool investment that help investors to diversify their portfolio by purchasing multiple assets with a single transaction. ETFs are different from mutual funds in that they trade like stocks throughout the day. You can purchase a single share of an ETF, just like a stock, and have more pricing control. This is a good starting point in investment because it diversifies your portfolio, and it is good when you are just starting out with a small amount.

7. Real Estate Investment Trusts

REITs are equities that are usually utilized by people looking to increase their portfolio's yield. These investment tools make it simple to own a piece of income-generating real estate. REITs can provide high yields, but like most high-return assets, they are riskier than lower-yielding options such as Treasury bonds.

Investment education is critical, as is avoiding investments you don't completely comprehend. Trust the advice of seasoned investors rather than "hot suggestions" from unreliable sources. Instead of commission-based financial counselors, seek independent financial advisors. Above all, diversify your assets.

How to start investing

If you're under the age of 18, you can open a custodial account with a financial institution. But if you're 18 or older, you can start your own account.

Custodial accounts are accounts that can be set up by parents, guardians, and other adults on behalf of minors. Custodial accounts are required since minors cannot engage in any financial transactions, such as creating stock trading and bank accounts, without adults.

One great way for you to invest is creating a custodial account. That can be your first step.

Let me break down for you the top custodial brokerage accounts into two classifications:

New and traditional custodial brokerage accounts

Let's begin with traditional. The following are the top conventional brokers that provide custodial brokerage accounts. Note that most have been around for decades:

1) Charles Schwab
2) E-Trade
3) Fidelity
4) Interactive Brokers
5) Ally Invest

Each stock trade used to cost a lot of money for these respected brokers. Also, they used to require big balances in brokerage accounts. They have all altered now to make purchasing and selling stock far less expensive. This is fantastic news for young investors like you.

There are newer online brokers who, through custodial brokerage accounts, offer excellent banking services for children. Some have only been around for a few years, but we are confident that many more will follow.

These companies specifically built their businesses and designed their apps to:

1) Attract parents who want to set up custodial accounts to help instruct their kids about money management, and
2) Attract young ones who want to have savings and investments. To put it another way, these businesses put parents and young investors/savers at the forefront of their branding and advertisements.

Here is a partial list of the newer companies that offer custodial brokerage accounts:

1) Greenlight
2) Loved Investing
3) Stockpile
4) Stash
5) Acorns

Several of these new custodial brokerage firms charge a small monthly fee for assisting young and beginning investors in putting together a portfolio or setting up extremely simple investing strategies.

Earlier, we discussed retirement funds. Most teenagers aren't thinking about retirement, but you should be. After decades of compounding, a small investment today might turn into a large sum.

A Roth IRA is an excellent place to start because it allows for tax-free growth and withdrawals in retirement. Here are some suggestions to help you begin planning and saving for their future.

The tax benefit of a Roth IRA is one of its most appealing features. A Roth IRA does not provide an immediate tax benefit like a standard IRA. Instead, your contributions and earnings will continue to grow tax-free indefinitely.

For teenagers, this usually works out well. Because most teenagers pay little or no income tax, this is the case. A teen's earnings qualify them for a Roth if they work during the summer or throughout the school year.

A custodial Roth IRA account for minors must be opened by an adult. In most states, this is 18 years old, whereas in others, it is 19 or 21 years old. These accounts are similar to traditional Roth IRAs. However, the minimum investment costs may be lower. Custodial Roth IRA accounts are available from many (but not all) brokers.

The adult manages the Roth IRA assets as custodian until the minor achieves the age of majority. The account is then transferred to the minor. A minor can continue to contribute to a Roth IRA and build a solid financial future, no matter how distant that future may appear.

You may also want to check out some of the investing apps. Be informed of the note fees and uses of each. Some that you can check out are M1 Finance and Acorns Early.

You may also do some researching on your own. The web includes a wealth of ideas about investments not just for adults but for youngsters like you as well.

Make your first investment

You have been given many stock options; it's time to choose which one to invest in.

Here are the best actions to take:

1) Determine Your Goals

Determining the goal of your portfolio is the first action when you select assets. Most people want to make money. That's why they invest, but there are investors who place more importance in having an income supplement upon retirement. This is for conservation of wealth or capital appreciation.

2) Keep Your Eyes Open

It's crucial to keep abreast of market news. You can do passive research including reading financial reports and news and following industry blogs written by people whose perspectives you find compelling. An investing thesis can be founded on a news item, an article, or even a blog post.

A simple observation can serve as the fundamental argument. For instance, you would notice that emerging market countries are developing new middle classes, which necessitate a greater choice of consumer goods. As a result, demand for particular items and commodities will increase.

3) Look and research on companies to choose from

There are three straightforward methods to do this:

a. Find exchange-traded funds (ETFs) that adhere to the performance of the industry you're interested in. You can examine the equities they hold. Search for "Industry X ETF" on Google, and the official ETF website will show you the fund's top holdings.

b. Use a screener to filter stocks based on particular factors like industry and sector. Buyers can have more options with screeners. Examples include sorting companies by dividend yield, market cap, and other important investment indicators.

c. For news and information on companies you've selected, search the blogosphere, financial press releases, and stock analysis articles. Always be cautious of what you read and consider both sides of an argument.

These aren't the only ways to choose a business, but they're a good place to start. Investors should think about the benefits and drawbacks of each technique.

It takes time to seek out professional perspectives through news sources, but it can pay off. It will help you learn more about the principles of the industry. It may also alert you to fascinating smaller companies that are not included in screeners or ETF holdings.

4) Pay attention to business presentations

It's time to look into investor presentations once you've learned that the industry of interest is a sound investment and you're familiar with the top players. They are not as detailed as financial statements, but they provide a general summary of how businesses make money and are easier to comprehend than 10-Q and 10-K reports.

These reports will also provide predictions for the company's and industry's future trends. You can narrow down your search by looking at company websites and presentations. The method is a more in-depth examination of a given company to determine whether it can surpass its industry competitors.

Once you have done these things and chosen your investment, how will you buy? One great option is through market order.

A market order is an immediate purchase or sale of a security. This form of order ensures that the order will be fulfilled, but not the price of fulfillment. A market order will typically execute at or near the current bid (sell order) or ask (buy order) price. Investors should keep in mind, however, that the last-traded price is not always the price at which a market order will be filled.

Now, I advise you to repeat until you build your portfolio. Stocks, bonds, and mutual/exchange-traded funds are examples of assets that can be included in an investing portfolio. Although, especially in the era of digital investing, this investment portfolio is considered more of an idea than a real space. It might be helpful for you to think of your assets as being under one metaphorical roof.

If you have a 401(k), an individual retirement account, and a taxable brokerage account, for example, you should consider all three accounts when selecting how to invest. You can hire a Robo-advisor or a financial advisor to manage your assets for you if you want to be fully hands-off with your portfolio.

You might ask what a Robo-advisor is. Robo-advisors, often known as automated investing services, design and manage your investment portfolio using computer algorithms and smart software. The services are available from automatic balance to tax efficiency, and they don't require much human interaction — though many providers do have human advisors on hand to answer issues.

Traditional portfolio management services frequently demand large balances, but Robo-advisors usually have low or no minimum requirements. Because of this, and because of their low fees, Robo-advisors allow you to get started very rapidly — in many cases, in minutes.

Why should you have one? A Robo-advisor can make your investing process easier. These online services make it easy to get started planning for your financial objectives by offering low-cost investment advice and account minimums of zero or minimal.

Consider the following factors when deciding whether a Robo-advisor is good for you:

1) Type of account.

The majority of Robo-advisors handle both taxable and retirement accounts. Some also handle trusts, and a select few assist you with your 401(k) plan (k).

2) Minimum investment requirements.

Some Robo-advisors have account minimums of $5,000 or more, although the majority have $500 or less.

3) Investment selection.

Low-cost exchange-traded funds (ETFs) and index funds, which are baskets of investments that try to mimic the behavior of an index make up the majority of Robo-advisors' portfolios. In addition to the Robo-management advisor's fee, you'll pay the costs imposed by those funds, known as expense ratios.

4) Portfolio recommendation.

When you first sign up with a Robo-advisor, you'll nearly always be asked to fill out a questionnaire that will analyze your risk tolerance, goals, and investing preferences. Robo-advisors usually have five to ten portfolio options, ranging from cautious to aggressive. The service's algorithm will suggest a portfolio based on your responses to these questions, but you should be able to reject it if you prefer a different alternative.

Dollar-cost averaging

DCA is an investment method wherein the total amount you are to invest is divided up into purchases at fixed intervals of a target asset in order to lessen the impact of volatility on the overall purchase. The acquisitions are made at regular intervals and regardless of the asset's price.

In fact, this method eliminates a lot of the tedious labor of trying to time the market in order to buy stocks at the optimal price, making it a convenient investing strategy that can help make investing less risky, less emotional, and less complicated.

Dollar-cost averaging can help you invest with less emotion. It compels you to invest the same (or nearly the same) amount regardless of market swings, potentially preventing you from succumbing to the desire to time the market.

When you average an investment dollar-cost, you buy more shares when the price is low and less shares when the price is high. Over time, this could result in a lower average price per share.

Dollar-cost averaging can help you limit your losses if the market falls. It works by putting money in gradually rather than all at once.

But there are some downsides to it. Dollar-cost averaging can help you reduce your risk. However, investors who use this method may forego potentially better returns.

If the market rises during the time you're dollar-cost averaging, you can miss out on the potential gains you could have made if you invested all at once.

You may incur higher brokerage fees if you use dollar-cost averaging. These charges may reduce your profits. Of course, you must be diligent with that money on the sidelines in order to invest it rather than eroding it with purchases. But despite all this, you need to remember that as teens, you are likely not having large lump sums to invest and will be investing as you earn your money.

It's recommended that you combine DCA with buy and hold investing. Buy and hold investors think that "time in the market" is a more prudent investing approach than "timing the market," and that buying investment assets and keeping them for lengthy periods of time can provide decent long-term returns despite the volatility associated with short-term periods. Absolute market timing, on the other hand, involves an investor purchasing and selling over shorter time periods with the goal of buying at low prices and selling at high prices.

The buy-and-hold investor will claim that holding a position for a longer period of time necessitates less frequent trading than other techniques. As a result, trading expenses are reduced, resulting in a higher overall net return on the investment portfolio.

Retirement Investment

Investing for your retirement may be an alien idea to you now, but I could not stress more the importance of this at this stage in your life.

Here are some reasons:

1) Create a habit of saving

The sooner you start saving, the more likely it will become a long-term habit. If you see your money grow in a retirement account as a teenager, you might be more likely to join an employer-sponsored 401(k) once you start working.

2) Learn time value of money

The lengthier money is invested and earns interest, the more value it will have in the future. For example, at age 15, you put $2,000 in a retirement account. It will be worth $126,290 at age 65, if we assume a modest rate of return of about 2.5% and a $100 monthly commitment.

3) Flexibility

The earlier you begin saving for retirement, the more investment options you will have. You will have more time to recover losses if equities fall due to economic conditions if you opt to focus on greater risk activities that can give larger returns on your money.

If you recall, I mentioned Roth IRAs. This is a good time as any to discuss with you what this is and how it compares to a traditional IRA.

Both a Roth IRA and a Traditional IRA are excellent retirement accounts you can consider even at this early stage in your life. However, there are some distinct differences between the two. Keep these in mind when deciding which account is best for your specific needs.

Here are a few essential distinctions to remember:

1) Tax contributions

In Roth IRAs, you can contribute after tax. Meanwhile, with traditional IRAs, you can do it pre-tax.

2) Eligibility

You are eligible for Roth if you have income earnings below a specific level. For traditional, anybody who has earned income is eligible.

3) Contribution

For Roth, contributions are after taxes. With tradition, it's pre-tax.

4) Withdrawal penalties

It's both penalty and tax-free after five years and at the age of 59½ for Roth. It's penalty-free for traditional but taxed as current income after the age of 59½.

Monitoring your investments

Now, it is imperative that you keep a close watch on your investments. Periodically evaluate your investments to ensure that you're on pace to meet your financial objectives and that you're satisfied with the investing risks.

There are several ways for you to keep track of your investments. And the great thing is that you have many ways to do it online. There are several programs you can download for this purpose.

Here are a few of the most common ones:

1) Client Portals

If you are a wealthy or high-net-worth individual, you most likely work directly with a financial advisor or an asset management firm. These days, it's customary for them to provide clients with internet portals that allow them to follow their entire financial lives, including "held away" assets at various firms. These portals are useful tools that make life easier, and they are frequently covered by the investment advising costs you pay your adviser.

2) Personal Capital

This method has become one of the most popular ways to track investments for investors who do not engage with a more traditional Registered Investment Advisor. The software-as-a-service generates graphs and charts that show holdings (income, portfolio, and spending). It can examine your assets and make a comparison of your performance to your preferred stock market index to determine your genuine exposure to specific firms across different accounts and institutions. It delves into your 401(k) plan to assist you to understand the mutual fund expense ratio you're paying on your retirement portfolio.

3) Morningstar.com

Morningstar.com subscribers can not only view their stock and mutual fund ratings, but they can also create online portfolios. It features a unique feature called X-Ray that none of the others have. This X-Ray tool allows you to enter your mutual funds, and it then breaks down the underlying equities held within each of those funds to show you your actual portfolio holdings.

4) Mint.com

Mint.com is another popular investment tracking tool that makes it possible to create account information from multiple institutions and have it all consolidated on one screen. You can create budgets for yourself, track how much you spend on different categories, track your investing costs, and compare your individual accounts to benchmarks like the S&P 500 or Dow Jones Industrial Average.

If you don't want the above methods, you can do it the old-fashioned way: through spreadsheets. You can use Microsoft Excel or Google spreadsheets.

If you want the software installed, here are a few options:

1) Quicken

The ordinary retail investor will find that the investment version of Quicken fits the majority of their requirements.

2) QuickBooks

The flexibility of using a typical accounting software application to handle their investment holdings will appeal to accountants or more knowledgeable investors who are familiar with GAAP known as the Generally Accepted Accounting Principles.

3) Fund Manager

Fund Manager is a software program that comes the closest to professional investment tracking for ordinary investors.

Don't be overwhelmed with all these options. All you need to do is study them and pick the one most suited for you.

Another thing you need to do is consistently rebalance your portfolio. Rebalancing your portfolio will allow you to stick to your initial asset allocation strategy while also allowing you to make any adjustments to your investment approach. Rebalancing, in essence, will assist you to stick to your investing plan regardless of market conditions, allowing you to stay within your risk tolerance levels.

Before ending this chapter, let me just provide you with some additional tips:

1) Start small. You don't want to overwhelm yourself.
2) Take it one step at a time; be patient.
3) Consider clubs and virtual trading.
4) Remember your tax obligations on unearned income.
5) Take note of the tax obligations under the kiddie tax.
6) Don’t invest in something you don’t understand.
7) Don’t fall for investment scams that seem too good to be true.
8) Keep learning about investing, stocks, etc. Keep abreast on things.

Next Steps

The most important thing for you to do is build up your investment knowledge. Have a thorough reflection on your investment goals and possibilities.

There may be some details provided to you in this chapter, but it's best that you stock up on what you know. Examine the various online brokerages and investing applications available to determine which one best suits your needs and interests.

Investing during your teen years is not impossible. This chapter showed you that. Now all you need to do is make it happen.

There's a lot to learn about investing, but it will come in handy all through your adulthood and into retirement. It will help you reach your financial goals faster and make sure your money keeps earning more money.

When you earn all this money, and start to plan to use it, you'll want to make sure it's safe and secure and that you don't lose it.

Chapter Ten

Protecting Yourself and Your Finances

While insurance protects your finances in case something happens to you, for the most part, it can't protect you from your mistakes and from being scammed. You need to do that yourself.

Your generation has grown up with smartphones and computers. But even if you are tech-savvy, you are not prone to be victimized.

Between 2017 and 2020, people aged 20 and below had the quickest scam victim growth rate. It was about 156% of all age brackets evaluated, according to Social Catfish, a social media research agency. According to the Federal Trade Commission, as of 2021, consumers lost more than $5.8 billion to fraud.

Untrustworthy individuals can scam investors in order to enrich themselves. Scammers are always coming up with new ways to deceive people. However, if you know what to look for, you may be able to avoid being a victim.

Financial pitfalls abound in life. It's easy to create financial mistakes, even with the greatest of intentions. The great news is that it's not too late to learn from your mistakes, and it's never too early to prevent them.

Financial Mistakes

No one is immune to making mistakes. If your parents or older adults are guilty of making them, someone younger like you is likely to commit mistakes as well.

Here are ten common financial mistakes you can make and certainly would want to avoid:

1) Having no plans or a budget

Failure to create a budget or financial plan is a typical financial mistake. A financial plan is a map of achieving your financial objectives. Setting SMART (specific, measurable, achievable, relevant, and time-bound) goals and having an investment and savings plan will get you there.

2) Overspending

Large fortunes are frequently lost dollar by dollar. When you buy that $5 cup of coffee, eat out, or order a pay-per-view movie, it may not seem like a huge thing, but it all adds up.

Dining out for $25 per week costs $1,300 per year, which may be put to an extra credit card, auto payment, or numerous more payments. If you're facing financial difficulties, avoiding this blunder is critical—after all, when you're barely just a couple of dollars away from bankruptcy or foreclosure, every dollar counts.

3) Making continuous payments

Cable TV, streaming platforms, and top-level gym memberships might force you to pay regularly while leaving you with nothing. When cash is tight or you merely want to save more, a somewhat more modest lifestyle can help you develop resources and safeguard yourself from financial hardship.

4) Paying late

When you fail on your mortgage or auto payments, you may find yourself in a difficult situation. Each time you go behind, you will have to pay late fees and some other charges. It could also harm your credit score, which could have long-term effects on your money.

5) Letting your credit report go unmonitored

Even though you're cautious with your credit, you should check your credit reports regularly to make sure you're liable for everything on them. Identity theft is on the rise, and it's also likely that a creditor or credit agency will make a mistake that will negatively impact your credit.

6) Utilizing home equity as a piggy bank

Using a HELOC or a home equity line of credit like a credit card will lead you to pay too much interest and hand ownership of your home to someone else. Your HELOC should be used carefully.

7) Living paycheck to paycheck

Overspending has a cumulative effect that puts people in a dangerous position where they need every dollar they make, and a delayed paycheck would be disastrous. The household personal savings rate in the United States was 9.4% in June 2021. Many people live paycheck to paycheck, and an unexpected problem can quickly turn into a crisis if you are not prepared.

8) Making financial decisions under pressure or fear

Another common blunder is to make a financial decision while you are afraid or under pressure. You may not evaluate all of your alternatives when you are scared, and you may wind up making a pricey mistake. It's critical to take a step back and think about all of your possibilities.

Another financial blunder is giving in to peer pressure to make a significant financial decision, such as purchasing a new automobile, purchasing a home, getting married, or having a child. You may not be prepared for these measures, and succumbing to peer pressure will not help you financially.

9) Living on borrowed money

Utilizing credit cards to buy necessities has become very common. Even though there's an increasing number of individuals who are willing to pay double-digit interest rates on fuel, food, and a variety of other products that are used long before the bill is fully paid, it isn't sound financial advice. Interest rates on your credit cards increase the cost of charged things significantly. Using credit might sometimes lead to you spending more than you make.

10) Not investing in your future

You may never be able to retire if you do not have enough money to work for you in the money market or through other types of investments. For a pleasant retirement, monthly deposits to designated retirement funds are essential.

It's easy to create financial mistakes, even with the greatest of intentions. The great news is that it's not too late to learn from your mistakes, and it's never too early to prevent them.

Financial Scams

When someone takes money or other assets from you through deception or illegal action, this is known as financial scam or fraud. Here are some of the most common financial scams/crimes you should know about:

1) Social media scams

Scams targeting teenagers are common on social media. Teenagers are social creatures, and recent epidemic lockdowns have aided in creating a perfect combination of teen anxiety and fraudster opportunity. Identity theft is a prevalent social media scam. Surveys or contests that ask for personal information are the most common, as is catfishing, in which a fraudster impersonates someone they are not and charms the victim to steal money, private details, or more.

2) Phishing

Phishing professionals send emails or messages that appear to be from banks, well-known retailers, or someone you know to trick you into sharing bank account or credit card details, login passwords, or personal information like your Social Security number.

3) Ransomware

Ransomware is a sort of malware that locks you out of your computer, smartphone, or tablet until you pay a ransom. Ransomware can spread to devices by opening a contaminated email attachment or clicking on a link to an infected file or website. Ransomware can attack a corporation's computer network or be disseminated via a contaminated flash drive.

4) Online shopping scams

Teens are significant internet spenders on high-end items. It seems too good to be true when you can get the newest gadget, or a luxury purse, for a quarter of the retail price. Unfortunately, it is precisely that: too good to be true. They are frequently duped into visiting suspicious links that take their money but sell them nothing, into revealing personal information for identity theft, or into clicking on links that download malware.

Another kind of this con involves knockoffs or counterfeit goods masquerading as the real deal.

5) Identity theft

It's one of the most common scams, and it's not just on social media. Websites, email, messaging apps, and pop-up windows are some of the other options. The naiveté of youngsters makes phishing for information much easier for would-be identity fraudsters. Young people are often unaware that they are disclosing personal information that could be used to commit identity theft.

6) Scholarship and grant scams

As college costs rise and students (and their parents) are concerned about paying for college, suspicion of unsolicited scholarships and grant offers may be less than it should be. These scams may be aimed at simple identity theft or a more direct attempt to charge for so-called private information about scholarships or free money that the general public is unaware of.

7) Debt collection scams

Fraudsters may masquerade as debt collectors to get you to pay for debts you don't own or have previously paid.

8) Multi leveling marketing (MLM)

MLM companies provide their products or services to individuals. That means you're selling to other people directly, whether from your home, a customer's home, or online, which makes it seem easy for teens to make money but most people who join genuine multi-level marketing companies make little or no money.

Some of them are in debt. People may feel they've entered a genuine MLM, but it turns out it was an illegal pyramid scheme that steals their money and leaves them in debt.

Keeping your finances secure

Now that you know some of the most prevalent scams and fraudulent issues you can be a victim of, it's imperative to know some tips to protect your money and yourself from these unlawful acts.

1) Never share your One Time PIN/Password (OTP)

The first line of defense against potential fraudsters is your One Time Password (OTP). Under no circumstances should you disclose your One Time Password (OTP) with anyone.

When you use their payment platform to make a purchase, pay, or withdraw money, most banks and payment firms can send you warnings. Please sign up for these immediate notifications; they can be bothersome at times, but they are necessary.

2) Never share your password

Do not disclose to anyone your password or jot it down anywhere. If you must, keep your list somewhere safe and secure. Using an app like Dashlane, can keep your passwords safe in one secure place.

When shopping online in public settings, be extra cautious to avoid accidentally disclosing your password.

3) Never share your reset password link

For fraudsters who have obtained your email ID through illegal means such as phishing or vishing, your reset password link is a potent tool. Please make sure your account's security questions are strong and consistent. If a fraudster can answer all of your security questions after a fast visit to your social media sites, a strong password is meaningless.

4) Set strong and unique passwords for your accounts

One of the simplest ways to safeguard your account is to choose a strong password. Strong passwords and PINs with digits, characters, and symbols are recommended.

Make each account's password distinct. That way, a single data leak won't compromise all of your accounts.

5) Make no banking transactions via unsecured public networks

The majority of public hotspots in public places such as airports, hotels, and restaurants lower their security standards to make it easier for visitors and travelers to access and use these networks. Fraudsters will be able to eavesdrop on these unsecured Wi-Fi networks and try to intercept your information simpler as a result.

6) Sign up for account notifications

Use any alert program supplied by your financial institution or credit card provider to its greatest potential. If there is odd or suspected behavior on your account, you may receive emails, SMS, phone calls, or all three. There's no reason why you shouldn't use this functionality.

7) Use smartphone apps with caution

Friends and family members may simply move money from one account to another, making money transfer and mobile payment apps increasingly popular. However, as convenient as this may seem, having a third-party digital access to your wallet carries significant hazards. Scammers and fraudsters have already hacked into several of these apps. Make sure your device is safe if you use apps like Venmo, Square Cash, or Apple Pay. Avoid syncing the app to your debit card or bank account if at all feasible, and instead use your credit card.

8) Keep receipts

Carrying these tiny scraps of paper around may not be convenient, but you'll thank yourself if something goes wrong with your account. Make a point of comparing your receipts to your monthly statements.

9) Keep an eye on your finances

Although credit and debit cards make shopping easier, it doesn't imply you should forget about each purchase once it's over. You should at the very least monitor your statements periodically and check your credit report once a year. You can review your account activity everyday using online banking to check your statements and transactions. Even if it's only for a minute a day, this will get you thinking about money and help you recognize mistakes quickly if something odd emerges.

10) Encrypt your data

When entering any confidential information, make sure to use an encrypted connection. If a connection is secure, the URL will begin with "https," and a small lock icon will appear in the address bar or the browser's status bar. Look attentively at the details regarding the SSL authentication certificate that has been issued to the site when you click on the lock symbol (you'll be able to see when the certificate was issued, who issued it, and for how long the certificate was issued).

11) Be cautious of possibly dangerous websites and questionable attachments

Avoid purchasing from retailers who have websites registered with free hosting providers. Don't click on attachments or links sent by unknown sources.

12) Protect yourself against viruses and other Internet security threats

Anti-malware software can protect you from computer viruses, worms, Trojan viruses, and other threats. Some anti-malware programs also feature advanced technology that gives extra layers of security to online buying and financing websites.

Now apart from protecting yourself from fraud and scams, you can take some measures in keeping your head above water with whatever financial issues you may encounter.

Let's look at debts. It would be best for you if you don't get caught up in debt. When things go bad (as they often do), those with less debt usually have the quickest time getting out. If you can't pay your expenses due to a job loss, sudden illness, or worldwide pandemic, it's likely due in part to your debt. You can carefully decide which bills you want to cancel as well as stick to a basic debt repayment plan until your credit record only shows good payment history.

Maintain a level head regardless of what's going on in the stock market. Trying to predict what the stock market will do next is like attempting to predict how long a rodeo cowboy would stay on the back of a bucking bronco. There may be warning signals that something is about to go wrong, but you never know when it will.

Sometimes, all these talks about finances, frauds, and stuff can be overwhelming. What you can do is find help. You can seek some professional advice.

A good financial advisor is worth his or her weight in gold. They can assist you fill in knowledge gaps, warn you when anything is concerning, and keep you on track. They'll also insist you invest in a method that protects your investments if you're planning to retire soon.

Next Steps

Don't just review for exams; review your finances as well. Find out ways how you can better protect them. You can work so hard to earn, save and grow your money, but with one stupid mistake, you can lose it all.

There will always be unscrupulous elements trying to get your money, so you always need to be on your guard and keep yourself updated on their sneaky methods.

This chapter reminds you how important your finances are. It's not enough that you learn how to spend, save, invest, and such. It's important to know the necessity of protecting your hard-earned money.

In good times and bad, the guidelines for protecting your money are the same. Although the world is in chaos, there are numerous strategies to safeguard your finances. Whatever the state of the economy, you can devise a strategy to protect yourself from unforeseen events.

By knowing how to protect your own finances, you may avoid becoming a statistic. You can protect your accounts and keep your money where it belongs by taking a few steps.

Conclusion

It is never too early to begin developing healthy financial habits. In fact, the sooner you are taught excellent financial habits, the more likely you are to become financially aware. This is a crucial life lesson in general. I know how good financial habits can set up a person for a better future; that's why I am sharing all this with you.

Some of you are very excited to become adults; you constantly think about what lies ahead. Yes, it's fun and rewarding, but you need the right foundation to face life's challenges. One challenge is handling money.

Your teen years are undoubtedly some of the most exciting and immediate milestones of your life. You will not only have the ability to make crucial life decisions, but you will have the grand opportunity to be in charge of your own finances.

In your quest to become financially knowledgeable and independent during your teen years, it's best that you start getting rid of false notions about money and other financial stuff. Throw these myths out the window and simply focus on cold hard facts about earning, spending, saving, and investing money. Jumpstarting your financial independence in this manner ensures your success.

You or your parents may worry that work might distract you from your studies. But having a job at this stage can provide you with lots of benefits.

Working allows you to develop skills and knowledge that would come in handy when you become older. In addition, it would help a lot for you to have money to spend on your wants and needs. Your parents would be so grateful if you have earnings that could alleviate some of their financial responsibilities. And I assure you, it is a great feeling when you know you can be of help.

Don't worry about getting a job. There are plenty of opportunities for you to try your hand at work. Just remember the tips that I provided earlier about finding work; you'll be good to go. Get the experience you need.

But once you have work and begin earning a salary, remember not to get too caught up with the idea of spending all of it. Don't get too carried away with shopping and throwing money on things that you don’t really need. Instill in yourself the value of budgeting. Making a budget is critical to your long-term prosperity and security.

Of course, you will have to spend your money at some point. You can indulge yourself. After all, you work hard for that money. Just always spend with caution.

Apply prioritization. Be reminded that bills and expenses should be prioritized in order of significance to satisfy fundamental demands, preserve your credit, and reduce financial stress. As a result, you can concentrate on cutting expenditures or increasing your revenue so that you can pay all of your payments on time and perhaps start saving for the future.

I cannot reiterate any further the importance of saving. You have to get rid of the thinking that you don't need to save since you are still young. You might say there are many years ahead for you to reach this endeavor. But there's no better time than the present. Just look at it this way – the sooner you start saving, the earlier you start enjoying your savings. You don't need to get to 100 years old to live off what you saved.

The advantages of saving money are pretty straightforward: it gives you the chance to live a more secure and satisfying life. If you have money saved up for emergency situations, you will be ready if something unexpected happens. If you have money put in place for discretionary spending, you become capable of taking some risks or trying new things.

Saving money allows you to have some left for more noteworthy transactions. This includes investments. Investing as a teen allows you to increase your wealth through compound interest and develop money management skills at an early age. You can also save money to pay for insurance. You may not know it yet, but insurance is such a help in cases of emergencies and unforeseen circumstances.

Hold off your horses when you become a credit card holder. Whether it's your first one or any succeeding ones, it can be easy to fall prey to unwise credit card spending. The power to buy stuff without having to pay for it all at the onset can be quite irresistible, but something you may regret. Your credit score matters.

With all these financial opportunities in front of you, you need to be vigilant. It's a top priority to protect yourself and your hard-earned money and investments at all costs.

Having effective money skills is critical because it provides you with a great foundation to efficiently manage your finances. Your financial decisions and actions lack a firm basis for success without it.

I wish I could have known all this information when I was your age. But you now have an opportunity to use all this to your advantage. Knowledge is power, as they say.

You have what it takes now. Your money skills that you learn as a teen can take you towards a more fulfilling and abundant adulthood.

This book has taught you a lot of things from budgeting your money to saving to investing. But there are many more lessons to be learned and many more steps to be taken. This book is just a first step. It's your battery to jumpstart your financial literacy and independence.

Don't allow yourself to be too complacent with what you know. Always find ways to harness your knowledge and skills about your finances. There is a wealth of information out there; it's all yours for the taking.

Keep learning; keep applying what you learned. Consider money as a serious aspect of your life.

Be money smart. Not when you're 40. Not even when you're 30.

Do it now!

Your adult self will thank you for it.

If you found this book helpful and think that it can help others like you who are trying to develop their financial skills at a young age, please leave a review. In doing so, you can help us reach others who may find value in the insights and advice in this book.

REFERENCES

5 Benefits of a Teenager Bank Account with Debit Card | Central Willamette CU - Albany, Corvallis, Lebanon & Salem. (n.d.). Central Willamete Credit Union. https://www.centralwcu.org/articles/5-benefits-teenager-bank-account-debit-card

5 Benefits of Teen Savings and Checking Accounts | Rivermark Community Credit Union. (n.d.). Rivermarkcu.Org. https://www.rivermarkcu.org/youth/resources/benefits-of-teen-savings-checking

6 Reasons Why a Teenager Should Get a Part-Time Job. (2020, April 16). Tough Nickel. https://toughnickel.com/finding-job/6-Reasons-Why-a-Teenager-Should-Get-a-Part-time-Job

7 Tips on How to Use a Credit Card Responsibly. (2021, March 21). Capital One. https://www.capitalone.com/learn-grow/money-management/tips-using-credit-responsibly/

Acton, B. (2017, February 28). *credit.com.* Credit.Com. https://www.credit.com/blog/how-high-school-students-can-start-building-credit-asap-166771/

Bank, M. S. (2019, July 26). *5 Common-Sense Money Management Tips for Teens*. Mercer Savings Bank. https://mercersavings.com/5-common-sense-money-management-tips-for-teens/

Barroso, A. (2022, February 26). *What Is Credit and Why Do You Need It?* NerdWallet. https://www.nerdwallet.com/article/finance/what-is-credit

Beattie, A. (2021, March 3). *10 Risks That Every Stock Faces*. Investopedia.

https://www.investopedia.com/articles/stocks/11/risks-every-stock-faces.asp

Benson, A. (2021, December 9). *Investment Portfolio: What It Is and How to Build a Good One*. NerdWallet. https://www.nerdwallet.com/article/investing/investment-portfolio

Best Custodial Brokerage Accounts for Kids. (n.d.). TeenVestor. https://www.teenvestor.com/best-custodial-brokerage-account-for-kids

Bessette, C. (2022, May 12). *What Do You Need to Open a Bank Account?* NerdWallet. https://www.nerdwallet.com/article/banking/how-to-open-a-bank-account-what-you-need

Blanco, L. T. (2020, February 1). *4 Tips to Help Teens Manage Money*. TODAY.Com. https://www.today.com/parenting-guides/4-tips-help-teens-manage-money-t177331

Bragg, S. (2022, March 10). *Cash payment definition.* AccountingTools. https://www.accountingtools.com/articles/cash-payment#:%7E:text=A%20cash%20payment%20is%20bills,through%20the%20accounts%20payable%20system.

Brennan, D. (2021, March 2). *Benefits of a Teenager Getting a Job.* Web MD. https://www.webmd.com/parenting/benefits-of-a-teenager-getting-a-job

Butsch, C. (2022, January 5). *Investing 101: How To Invest As A Teenager.* Money Under 30. https://www.moneyunder30.com/how-to-invest-as-a-teenager

Buchenau, Z. (2020, December 31). *Is It Better To Keep Money In The Bank Or At Home?* Be The Budget. https://bethebudget.com/keep-money-in-the-bank-or-at-home/

C. (2019, February 13). *Importance of Having Short and Long Term Goals.* Columbia College Calgary. https://www.columbia.ab.ca/importance-short-long-term-goals/#:%7E:text=If%20you%20have%20a%20long,keep%20moving%20towards%20your%20goals.

Cain, S. (2022, March 23). *10 Common Financial Mistakes.* Prosper Blog. https://www.prosper.com/blog/10-common-financial-mistakes/

Chen, J. (2022, January 13). *Debt*. Investopedia. https://www.investopedia.com/terms/d/debt.asp

Cherry, K. (2021, April 25). *How Does the Placebo Effect Work?* Verywell Mind. https://www.verywellmind.com/what-is-the-placebo-effect-2795466

Clifford, E. (2021, February 11). *16 Young And Successful Entrepreneurs Who Prove That Age Is Nothing but a Number*. Lifehack. https://www.lifehack.org/588440/16-young-and-successful-entrepreneurs-who-prove-that-age-is-nothing-but-a-number#:%7E:text=1.,was%20only%2019%20years%20old.

Comai-Legrand, L. (2019, April 9). *Should Teens Carry a Credit Card?* First Alliance.

https://www.firstalliancecu.com/blog/should-teens-carry-a-credit-card

10 Common Financial Scams | UW Credit Union Winter 2019. (n.d.). UW Credit Union. https://www.uwcu.org/technology/articles/10-common-financial-scams/

Cornfield, J. (2020, March 6). *You bring lunch to work every day yet you're still not rich. Here's why*. CNBC. https://www.cnbc.com/2020/03/06/how-investing-is-the-link-between-good-financial-habits-and-wealth.html

Curtis, G. (2021, June 20). *Understanding Different Loan Types*. Investopedia. https://www.investopedia.com/articles/pf/07/loan_types.asp

Daugherty, G. (2022, March 29). *Can Teenagers Invest in Roth IRAs?* Investopedia. https://www.investopedia.com/can-teenagers-invest-in-roth-iras-4770663

Delbridge, E. (2022, May 17). *What You Need to Know About Car Loans*. The Balance. https://www.thebalance.com/the-basics-of-car-loans-4797802#citation-

DeMatteo, M. (2022, April 25). *Here's the difference between secured and unsecured loans*. CNBC. https://www.cnbc.com/select/secured-loans-vs-unsecured-loans/#:%7E:text=Secured%20loans%20require%20that%20you,the%20lender%20considers%20your%20financials).

DeMatteo, M. (2021, July 15). *Should Gen Z be taking on more student loan debt? The decision's getting "harder and harder," says an economist*. CNBC. https://www.cnbc.com/select/are-student-loans-worth-it/

DeMarco, J. (2021, November 19). *How To Talk to Your Teen About Debt*. The Balance.

https://www.thebalance.com/how-to-talk-to-your-teen-about-debt-5202023

DeNicola, L. (2022, January 14). *What can I do if my loan is in default?* Credit Karma. https://www.creditkarma.com/advice/i/what-happens-if-you-default-on-a-loan

Dieker, N. (2022, January 14). *How to help your kids build credit*. Bankrate. https://www.bankrate.com/finance/credit-cards/educating-teens-about-credit/

Donovan, W. (2021, November 10). *Why Diversification Is Important to Your Portfolio*. The Balance. https://www.thebalance.com/the-importance-of-diversification-3025567

Doyle, A. (2021, August 5). *25 Easy Part-Time Jobs to Boost Your Income*. The Balance Careers. https://www.thebalancecareers.com/part-time-jobs-to-boost-income-4126475

Dowshen, S. (2018, July). *Health Insurance Basics (for Teens)* - Nemours KidsHealth. Kids Health. https://kidshealth.org/en/teens/insurance.html

E. (2021, June 13). *10 Things Teenagers Waste Money on*. Teen Finance Today. https://teenfinancetoday.com/10-things-teenagers-waste-money-on/

Egan, M. (2016, July 26). *16-year-old made $43,000 on these stocks in 3 years*. CNNMoney. https://money.cnn.com/2016/07/26/investing/16-

year-old-investor-tesla-netflix-sudarshan-sridharan/index.html

Encouraging Your Teen to Consider Saving for Retirement - Northwest Bank. (2021, March 3). Northwest Bank. https://www.nw.bank/newsroom/education/encouraging-your-teen-to-consider-saving-for-retirement

Farrington, R. (2020, November 11). *5 Things Your Millionaire Neighbor Isn't Telling You.* The College Investor. https://thecollegeinvestor.com/5656/5-millionaire-neighbor-telling/

Farrington, R. (2021, July 5). Alternatives To Student Loans To Pay For College Without Debt. The College Investor. https://thecollegeinvestor.com/1684/alternatives-to-student-loans/

Farrington, R. (2022, April 14). *Should Students Still Get Student Loans To Pay For College?* Forbes. https://www.forbes.com/sites/robertfarrington/2021/03/17/should-students-still-get-student-loans-to-pay-for-college/?sh=a2eaa504dbc9#open-web-0

Frobes. (n.d.). *Profile.* Retrieved from Forbes: https://www.forbes.com/profile/warren-buffett/?sh=1fe1789f4639

Fowler, J. (2022, April 12). *10 Common Scams Targeted at Teens.* Investopedia.

https://www.investopedia.com/financial-edge/1012/common-scams-targeted-at-teens.aspx#toc-3-identity-theft

Gavin, M. (2019, February). *5 Reasons to Look for a Summer Job (for Teens)* - Nemours KidsHealth. Kids Health. https://kidshealth.org/en/teens/5-summer-job.html

George, D. (2021, September 2). *4 Ways To Protect Your Money -- No Matter What's*

Going On With the Economy. The Motley Fool. https://www.fool.com/the-ascent/personal-finance/articles/4-ways-to-protect-your-money-no-matter-whats-going-on-with-the-economy/

GOBankingRates. (2021, June 7). *13 Blue-Collar Jobs That Turned People Into Millionaires*. https://www.gobankingrates.com/money/jobs/blue-collar-jobs-turned-people-into-millionaires/

Gocardless Team. (2022, May 31). *What is Direct Debit? A guide for payers*. GoCardless. https://gocardless.com/guides/intro-to-direct-debit/guide-for-payers/

Gobler, E. (2021, November 15). *Investing Guide for Teens (and Parents)*. The Balance. https://www.thebalance.com/investing-guide-for-teens-and-parents-4588018

Gobler, E. (2021, September 30). *What Teens and Parents Need To Know To Start Investing*. The Balance. https://www.thebalance.com/prepare-teen-first-investment-5203666

Gordon, A. (2018, October 22). *Why Does Budgeting Hurt So Much??!!* Connect Wealth.

https://www.connectwealth.com/why-does-budgeting-hurt-so-much/

Grab Philippines. (n.d.). *How to avoid financial scams, fraud and theft*. Grab PH. https://www.grab.com/ph/pay/security/how-to-avoid-financial-scams-fraud-and-theft/

Gran, B. (2020, April 10). *How To Automate Your Savings*. Forbes Advisor. https://www.forbes.com/advisor/banking/savings/how-to-automate-your-savings/

Gray, E. (2021, July 8). *Needs Vs. Wants: How to Tell the Difference*. Abilene Teachers Federal Credit Union. https://www.abileneteachersfcu.org/blog/needs-vs-wants-how-to-tell-the-difference/#:%7E:text=Defining%20needs%20and%20wants,while%20wants%20include%20everything%20else.

Grossman, A. L. (2022, April 2). *41 Things to Save Up for as a Teenager (Cool & Practical)*. Money Prodigy. https://www.moneyprodigy.com/things-to-save-up-for-as-teenager/

Grossman, A. L. (2022, March 14). *9 Reasons to Save Money as a Teenager (Use these Talking Points)*. Money Prodigy. https://www.moneyprodigy.com/reasons-to-save-money-as-a-teenager/

Guide to Starting a Business in High School For Teens - Crimson Education NZ. (2021, July 20). Crimson

Education. https://www.crimsoneducation.org/nz/blog/extracurriculars/high-school-entrepreneurship/

Hagen, D. (2020, November 20). *Why You Should Be Careful with Debt*. MoneyHealthSolutions. https://www.moneyhealthsolutions.com/post/be-careful-with-debt

Hayes, E. (2018, October 23). *The importance of money skills for kids*. Familyfriendlyhq.Ie. https://www.familyfriendlyhq.ie/parenthood/the-importance-of-money-skills-for-kids-2459/#:%7E:text=Money%20skills%20are%20vital%20for,independent%20as%20they%20grow%20older.

Hayes, A. (2022, March 13). *Dollar-Cost Averaging (DCA)*. Investopedia. https://www.investopedia.com/terms/d/dollarcostaveraging.asp#:%7E:text=Dollar%2Dcost%20averaging%20(DCA)%20is%20an%20investment%20strategy%20in,price%20and%20at%20regular%20intervals.

Hein, D. (2022, May 9). *Do You Need an Emergency Savings Fund? | Thrivent*. Thrivent.Com. https://www.thrivent.com/insights/budgeting-saving/myth-buster-do-i-need-an-emergency-savings-fund

Higuera, V. P. (2022, May 28). *How to Set Up a Savings Account for a Teenager*. MyBankTracker.

https://www.mybanktracker.com/savings/faq/how-to-set-up-a-savings-account-for-a-teenager-297534

How to Invest as a Teenager or a Minor. (n.d.). TeenVestor. https://www.teenvestor.com/7steps

Indeed Editorial Team. (2022, June 3). *15 Best Jobs for Teens*. Indeed Career Guide. https://www.indeed.com/career-advice/finding-a-job/best-jobs-for-teens

How to Manage Your Monthly Bills | Manage Your Bills. (2022, May 18). Mid Penn Bank. https://midpennbank.com/how-to-manage-your-monthly-bills/

How to write a check. (n.d.). Huntington. https://www.huntington.com/learn/checking-basics/how-to-write-a-check

Importance Of Saving For Retirement Early. (2021, December 17). Insular Life. https://www.insularlife.com.ph/articles/importance-of-saving-for-retirement-early-00000087

Irby, L. (2021, November 11). *What You Need to Know When Taking out a Personal Loan*. The Balance. https://www.thebalance.com/know-about-personal-loans-960025

Irby, L. (2022, January 13). *9 Attractive Benefits of a Good Credit Score*. The Balance. https://www.thebalance.com/having-good-credit-score-960528

J. (2021, October 7). *10 Tips On Budgeting For Teens in 2022.* Teen Financial Freedom. https://teenfinancialfreedom.com/10-tips-on-budgeting-for-teens/

Johnson, P. (2022, May 29). *Crafting Layered Stories for Filipnx People in Hollywood: A Conversation with Actor, Writer, and Director Jenn Santos*. GREY Journal. https://greyjournal.net/hustle/inspire/top-10-teen-entrepreneurs-to-watch-in-2020/#rb-Cory-Nieves-Age-16

Kaspersky. (2021, January 13). *Protecting Your Money - Security Tips*. Www.Kaspersky.Com. https://www.kaspersky.com/resource-center/preemptive-safety/money-online

Kennon, J. (2022, January 6). *The Easiest Ways to Track Investments*. The Balance. https://www.thebalance.com/what-are-the-easiest-ways-to-track-my-investments-357627

Kurt, D. (2021, June 11). *The Side Effects of Bad Credit*. Investopedia. https://www.investopedia.com/the-side-effects-of-bad-credit-4769783

Kurt, D. (2022, February 9). *Emergency Funds*. Investopedia. https://www.investopedia.com/terms/e/emergency_fund.asp

Kurtuy, A. (2022, January 4). *30+ Jobs for Teenagers (Where & How To Look)*. Novorésumé. https://novoresume.com/career-blog/jobs-for-teens

Lake, R. (2022, January 2). *Want a Better Credit Score? Here's How to Get It*. Investopedia. https://www.investopedia.com/how-to-improve-your-credit-score-4590097

Lake, R. (2022, March 15). *Credit Cards 101: How to Use Them to Make Purchases*. Investopedia. https://www.investopedia.com/how-to-use-a-credit-card-5069558

Lewis, F. (2013, July 25). 6 Reasons Why Should Teenagers Start Working Earlier- Infographic. Job Cluster. https://www.jobcluster.com/blog/teenagers-should-start-working-earlier/

Lexington Law. (2022, March 25). *Teen spending habits in 2022*. https://www.lexingtonlaw.com/blog/credit-cards/teen-spending-habits.html

Li, H. (2020, May 4). *8 Reason Why Your Teen should work*. Medium. https://medium.datadriveninvestor.com/8-reason-why-your-teen-should-work-dfc8a9a1c3b6

Little, K. (2021, April 11). *Understanding Risk and Reward in Investing*. The Balance. https://www.thebalance.com/understanding-risk-3141268

Lisa, A. (2021, June 7). *13 Blue-Collar Jobs That Turned People Into Millionaires*. GOBankingRates. https://www.gobankingrates.com/money/jobs/blue-collar-jobs-turned-people-into-millionaires/

Lynkova, D. (2022). *28 Millionaire Statistics: What Percentage of Americans Are Millionaires?* Retrieved from spendmenot.com: https://spendmenot.com/blog/what-percentage-of-americans-are-millionaires/

M. (2022, April 6). *Budgeting for Teens: 14 Tips For Growing Your Money Young*. MintLife Blog. https://mint.intuit.com/blog/budgeting/budgeting-for-teens/

Marquit, M. (2022, May 9). *Common Student Loan Alternatives to Consider*. LendEDU. https://lendedu.com/blog/common-student-loan-alternatives

Marquit, M. (2021, September 7). *5 Questions to Ask Before You Buy Something | Spending Tips + Advice*. Good Financial Cents®. https://www.goodfinancialcents.com/5-questions-to-ask-yourself-before-you-buy-something/

McClanahan, A. (2019, July 10). *How To Use Checkbooks - And Are They Even Still Relevant?* Money Under 30. https://www.moneyunder30.com/how-to-use-checkbooks

McKay, D. R. (2019, May 25). *Here Are the Top Tips to Help Teens Survive Their First Jobs*. The Balance Careers. https://www.thebalancecareers.com/tips-for-teens-who-toil-524900

Mind Tools Content Team. (n.d.). *SMART Goals: How to Make Your Goals Achievable.* Mind Tools. https://www.mindtools.com/pages/article/smart-goals.htm

Mobile phone debt: Can't afford to pay your bill? (n.d.). Step Change. https://www.stepchange.org/debt-info/mobile-phone-debt.aspx#:%7E:text=If%20you%20don't%20pay,the%20contract%20will%20be%20cancelled.

Moffatt, N. (2021, September 6). *9 Benefits of Saving Money in the Bank.* The Financial Geek. https://thefinancialgeek.com/blog/benefits-of-saving-money-in-bank/

Morgan, T. (2022, April 22). *The Pros & Cons of Teens Getting Jobs –.* TeenLife. https://www.teenlife.com/blog/pros-cons-teens-getting-jobs/

Morin, A. (2021, April 3). *What Are the Best Part-Time Jobs for Teens?* Verywell Family. https://www.verywellfamily.com/the-pros-and-cons-of-afterschool-jobs-for-teens-2610471

Muller, C. (2021, November 29). *How To Spend Money Wisely---A Guide For Teens.* Money Under 30. https://www.moneyunder30.com/how-to-spend-money-wisely-for-teens

Muller, C. (2022, June 2). *The 8 Most Important Employee Rights Teens Should Know.* Money Under 30.

https://www.moneyunder30.com/important-employee-rights-teens-should-know\

Muller, C. (2022, March 31). *Budgeting for teens: grow your money while you're young*. Money Under 30. https://www.moneyunder30.com/budgeting-for-teens

Multi-Level Marketing Businesses and Pyramid Schemes. (2022, March 7). Consumer Advice. https://consumer.ftc.gov/articles/multi-level-marketing-businesses-pyramid-schemes

Murphy, A. (2021, April 8). *10 Part-Time Jobs for Students.* Keystone Bachelor Studies. https://www.bachelorstudies.com/article/10-part-time-jobs-for-students/

Mythbusters: I Don't Need an Emergency Fund. (n.d.). My Max. Retrieved June 3, 2022, from https://www.mymax.com/learn-and-plan/advice-articles/mythbusters-i-dont-need-an-emergency-fund

MyBankTracker. (n.d.). *About MyBankTracker Company.* https://www.mybanktracker.com/blog/find-my-answers/6-benefits-paying-bills-early-14036

Norris, E. (2021, July 28). *Top 10 Most Common Financial Mistakes.* Investopedia. https://www.investopedia.com/personal-finance/most-common-financial-mistakes/#toc-3-living-on-borrowed-money

Nuggets, M. (2022, January 22). *7 Reasons You Need to Set Financial Goals.* Money Nuggets.

https://www.moneynuggets.co.uk/important-to-set-financial-goals/

Oneil, E. (2021, October 25). *Learn About 5 Different Accounts Your Bank Offers*. The Balance. https://www.thebalance.com/types-of-bank-accounts-315458

Opening a Bank Account for Teens. (2022, February 23). Capital One. https://www.capitalone.com/bank/money-management/banking-basics/bank-account-for-teens/

O'Shea, A. (2022, January 25). *What Is a Robo-Advisor and Is One Right for You?* NerdWallet. https://www.nerdwallet.com/article/investing/what-is-a-robo-advisor

O'Shea, B. (2022, April 5). *How to Improve Credit Fast*. NerdWallet. https://www.nerdwallet.com/article/finance/raise-credit-score-fast

Overholt, M. (2022, March 31). *What is a mortgage? Basics for first-time home buyers*. Mortgage Rates, Mortgage News and Strategy : The Mortgage Reports.

https://themortgagereports.com/19098/what-is-a-mortgage-and-how-does-it-work

Pinkasovitch, P. (2022, January 9). *How to Pick a Stock: Basic Best Practices for New Investors*. Investopedia. https://www.investopedia.com/articles/basics/11/how-to-pick-a-stock.asp

Pritchard, J. (2022, January 24). *Compound Interest*. The Balance. https://www.thebalance.com/compound-interest-4061154

Pritchard, J. (2022, April 4). *How To Open a Bank Account for a Minor*. The Balance. https://www.thebalance.com/bank-accounts-for-people-under-18-315365

Rawhide Youth Services. (2021, April 14). *9 teen job etiquette tips*. https://www.rawhide.org/blog/teen-issues/teen-job-etiquette/

Rebalance Your Portfolio to Stay on Track. (2022, January 19). Investopedia. https://www.investopedia.com/investing/rebalance-your-portfolio-stay-on-track/#:%7E:text=Rebalancing%20your%20portfolio%20will%20help,to%20your%20risk%20tolerance%20levels.

Reporting, B. (2022). Bloomburg Billionaires Index. Retrieved from Bloomburg: https://www.bloomberg.com/billionaires/profiles/mark-e-zuckerberg/?leadSource=uverify%20wall

Ronis, H. (2022, April 26). *How to Start a Business As a Teenager*. wikiHow. https://www.wikihow.com/Start-a-Business-As-a-Teenager

Roth vs. Traditional. (n.d.). Schwab Brokerage. https://www.schwab.com/ira/understand-iras/roth-vs-tradira#:%7E:text=With%20a%20Roth%20IRA%2C%2

0you,current%20income%20after%20age%2059%C2%BD.

Sabatier, G. (2022, January 28). *Best Online Jobs for Teens in 2022*. Millennial Money. https://millennialmoney.com/online-jobs-for-teens/

Sato, G. (2020, October 10). *4 Simple Habits That Build Good Credit*. Experian. https://www.experian.com/blogs/ask-experian/what-are-good-credit-habits/

support@workethic.org. (2018, October 16). *Why It's Important for Young People to Have Part-Time Jobs*. The Center for Work Ethic Development. https://workethic.org/why-its-important-for-young-people-to-have-part-time-jobs/

Sheppard, R. (2015, July 31). *10 Personal Finance Apps For Teens And Young Adults*. Yahoo Finance. https://finance.yahoo.com/news/10-personal-finance-apps-teens-113650850.html

Shiv, B., Carmon, Z., & Ariely, D. (n.d.). *Placebo Effects of Marketing Actions: Consumer May Get What they Pay For*. Stanford Graduate School of Business. Retrieved June 3, 2022, from https://www.gsb.stanford.edu/faculty-research/publications/placebo-effects-marketing-actions-consumer-may-get-what-they-pay

Shroll, L. (2022, April 11). *Future Visualization: How to Get from Now to Your Ideal Future.* Project OTY. https://www.projectoty.com/visualize-your-future-self/

Smith, L. (2021, April 29). *Good Debt vs. Bad Debt: What's the Difference?* Investopedia. https://www.investopedia.com/articles/pf/12/good-debt-bad-debt.asp

Spending Money Quotes. (n.d.). BrainyQuote. https://www.brainyquote.com/topics/spending-money-quotes

Suknanan, J. (2021, August 27). *Automating your savings will help you save more—here's the psychological reason why*. CNBC. https://www.cnbc.com/select/present-bias-why-automating-your-savings-works/

Tanner, M. (2011, November 8). *The Real "1 Percent."* Cato.Org. https://www.cato.org/commentary/real-1-percent#:~:text=Roughly%2080%20percent%20of%20millionaires,involved%20in%20banking%20or%20finance.

Teens and Emergency Funds. (2015, June 9). CBN.Com - The Christian Broadcasting Network. https://www1.cbn.com/teens-and-emergency-funds

Top 10 Advantages Teen Entrepreneurs Have While Commencing a Business. (2016, October 28). Entrepreneur. https://www.entrepreneur.com/article/284415

Top Reasons to start Investing at an early age - Axis Bank. (n.d.). Axis Bank. https://www.axisbank.com/progress-with-us/invest/top-reasons-to-start-investing-at-an-early-age

The best ways to pay bills | MoneyHelper. (n.d.). MaPS. https://www.moneyhelper.org.uk/en/everyday-money/budgeting/the-best-ways-to-pay-bills

The Family Money Team. (2022, February 1). *Creating a business plan with your teens*. Verizon. https://www.verizon.com/solutions-and-services/family-money/blog/posts/creating-a-business-plan-with-your-teens/

TheMint.org - Tips For Teens - What is the Stock Market? (n.d.). TheMint.Org. https://www.themint.org/teens/what-is-the-stock-market.html

TheMint.org - Tips For Teens - Risks & Rewards. (n.d.). TheMint.Org. https://www.themint.org/teens/risk-and-rewards.html

TheMint.org - Tips For Teens - Decoding Your Paycheck. (n.d.). TheMint.Org. https://www.themint.org/teens/decoding-your-paycheck.html

The Pros and Cons of Dollar-Cost Averaging | FINRA.org. (2022, May 24). FINRA. https://www.finra.org/investors/insights/dollar-cost-averaging

Thune, K. (2021, November 3). *How to Choose the Best Investment Strategies for You*. The Balance. https://www.thebalance.com/what-is-your-investment-style-2466436

Types of Orders | Investor.gov. (n.d.). Investor.Gov. https://www.investor.gov/introduction-investing/investing-basics/how-stock-markets-work/types-orders#:%7E:text=A%20market%20order%20is%20an,for%20a%20buy%20order)%20price.

United Bank & Trust Company. (n.d.). *Teens Encouraged to Consider Saving for Retirement*. https://www.ubtc.net/error.php?path=/handlers/request_handler.php

VanSomeren, L. (2021, July 17). *11 Disadvantages of Cash*. The Qube Money Blog. https://blog.qubemoney.com/11-disadvantages-of-cash/

Ways to Improve your Credit Score and Good Credit Habits – Wells Fargo. (n.d.). Wells Fargo. https://www.wellsfargo.com/goals-credit/smarter-credit/improve-credit/good-credit-habits/#:%7E:text=Contribute%20to%20an%20emergency%20fund,expenses%2C%20if%20your%20situation%20changes.

What Does a Millionaire Look Like? (2013, December 29). Myatt & Bell P.C. https://www.myattandbell.com/millionaire-like/

What Teens Should Know About Good Debt & Bad Debt. (2021, August 5). Get Schooled. https://getschooled.com/article/5785-good-debt-vs-bad-debt/

When do I need to start investing for my retirement? (n.d.). Money. https://money.cnn.com/retirement/guide/investing_basics.moneymag/index3.htm

Why Is Credit Important? (2021, August 1). Capital One. https://www.capitalone.com/learn-grow/money-management/why-credit-is-important/

Williams, G. (2019, May 31). *What Teens Must Know Before Starting a First Job*. U.S News. https://money.usnews.com/careers/applying-for-a-job/articles/what-teens-must-know-before-starting-a-first-job

Wise, J. (2022, March 22). *The Importance Of Money Security: 5 Tips To Protect Yourself.* Kasasa. https://www.kasasa.com/blog/identity-theft/5-protection-tips

With Me, J.-M. (2022, March 17). *7 Helpful Questions to Ask Yourself Before Buying Anything*. Minimise With Me. http://minimisewithme.com/7-questions/

Wu, J. (2021, July 12). *What are the consequences of a late payment on a credit card?* ValuePenguin. https://www.valuepenguin.com/credit-cards/what-happens-if-late-payment-credit-card

Zippia. (2022, September). *Zippia Careers* . Retrieved from What is a House Sitter?: https://www.zippia.com/house-sitter-jobs/

https://www.localwise.com/a/137-21-best-part-time-jobs-for-teens-and-high-school-students

https://www.ubtc.net/resources/news/teens-encourage-to-consider-saving-for-reitrement

Made in United States
Troutdale, OR
05/04/2024